THE
SAS
IN 1943

OPERATIONS IN SICILY AND ITALY

THE SAS IN 1943

OPERATIONS IN SICILY AND ITALY

GAVIN MORTIMER

Pen & Sword

MILITARY

AN IMPRINT OF PEN & SWORD BOOKS LTD.
YORKSHIRE – PHILADELPHIA

First published in Great Britain in 2024 by
PEN AND SWORD MILITARY
An imprint of
Pen & Sword Books Ltd
Yorkshire – Philadelphia

ISBN 978 1 39904 522 3

A CIP catalogue record for this book is available from the British Library

Typeset in Times New Roman 11.5/15 by SJmagic DESIGN SERVICES, India.
Printed and bound in the UK by CPI Group (UK) Ltd.

Pen & Sword Books Ltd incorporates the imprints of Pen & Sword Archaeology, Atlas, Aviation, Battleground, Discovery, Family History, History, Maritime, Military, Naval, Politics, Social History, Transport, True Crime, Claymore Press, Frontline Books, Praetorian Press, Seaforth Publishing and White Owl

For a complete list of Pen & Sword titles please contact

PEN & SWORD BOOKS LIMITED
George House, Units 12 & 13, Beevor Street, Off Pontefract Road, Barnsley, South Yorkshire, S71 1HN, England
E-mail: enquiries@pen-and-sword.co.uk
Website: www.pen-and-sword.co.uk

or

PEN AND SWORD BOOKS
1950 Lawrence Rd, Havertown, PA 19083, USA
E-mail: uspen-and-sword@casematepublishers.com
Website: www.penandswordbooks.com

Contents

Introduction

On 12 January 1943, Lieutenant Colonel David Stirling, commanding officer of the 1st Special Air Service Regiment (1SAS) was at Bir-el-Gheddafia in north-west Libya. Eighteen months earlier, he and his eldest brother, Bill, had formed the SAS, and what had begun life as a force of six officers and sixty men had grown into a regiment.

David Stirling felt the pressure of command. He had spent some of the previous November in a Cairo hospital, suffering from conjunctivitis and desert sores, exacerbated by nervous exhaustion. Upon his release, however, he was determined to make up for lost time, particularly as in his absence his second-in-command, Major Blair 'Paddy' Mayne, had led A Squadron of 1SAS in a series of spectacular raids against the Axis forces as they withdrew west from the front line at El Alamein.

Stirling resumed command of B Squadron, comprised predominantly of new recruits to 1SAS, and in late November he headed west from Cairo into the Libyan desert to begin offensive operations. It was not a successful period. Several of his inexperienced officers were killed or captured, a number of whom were known personally to Stirling – including Pat Hore-Ruthven, Peter Oldfield and Carol Mather.

Stirling had returned to the SAS base at Kabrit, 80 miles east of Cairo, for Christmas, but he was intent on returning 'Up the Blue' – as the SAS called the desert – in the new year. His plan was to lead a small raiding party west from Tripoli, attacking enemy lines of communication as well as reconnoitring the terrain for the Eighth Army. The intelligence provided would assist in the advance into Tunisia. Above all, it was Stirling's ambition to be the first soldier from the Eighth Army to link with the British First Army as it advanced east from Algeria after the Operation *Torch* landings. He would achieve his aim by taking the most direct route, driving through the Gabes Gap, a geographical bottleneck between the Mediterranean Sea and the Shotte Djerid, the largest salt lake in the Sahara Desert.

Senior officers had their reservations about the proposal. When Brigadier George Davy, Director of Military Operations in Cairo, learned of the route Stirling planned to take into Tunisia, he expressed his concern. 'I said he was going into an area where the natives were known to be hostile and that he would be captured,' Davy recalled. 'I suggested he should take a wider sweep. However, he was obstinate as usual.'

Bill (left) and David Stirling, co-founders of the SAS, photographed at Bill's wedding in December 1940.

The two most experienced officers remaining in B Squadron were French, Lieutenant François Martin and Captain Augustin Jordan, members of the contingent who had joined the SAS twelve months earlier. They rendezvoused with Stirling at Bir-el-Gheddafia, and at dawn on 15 January, Stirling and Martin set off, crossing into Tunisia just north of Ghadames. Twenty-four hours later, Captain Jordan followed the same route. They rendezvoused on 21 January a few miles south of Bir Soltane, Stirling instructing the two French officers to lead their patrols in attacks against enemy lines of communications between Sfax and Gabes.

A few hours later, Stirling's patrol drove north. There were fifteen men in total, travelling in five jeeps, one of which was driven by Corporal Reg Redington, a gunner who had been awarded the Distinguished Conduct Medal in 1941. 'It was exhausting work,' remembered Redington.

Above: *David Stirling was captured as he slept in a Tunisian wadi by German special forces, seen here posing with Stirling's jeep.*

Left: *Paddy Mayne was a brilliant guerrilla fighter who assumed command of 1SAS after David Stirling's capture.*

Alongside Redington was Lieutenant Mike Sadler, a superb navigator who had joined the SAS a year earlier from the Long Range Desert Group, the pioneers of British special forces in the desert. Sadler recalled:

> 'We went for the direct route through Gabes Gap and set off north to Shotte Djerid, a salt lake. We didn't cross the Shotte; there's a gap of about 20 miles between Gabes and the Shotte and we

Above left: *Mike Sadler was a superb navigator who joined the SAS from the Long Range Desert Group.*

Above right: *David Stirling's capture in January 1943 allowed Bill Stirling and Paddy Mayne to exert their influence on the SAS.*

> went through that. But the day before we went through the Gap a Storch [reconnaissance plane] came over and I think must have spotted us.'

Stirling's patrol passed through the Gabes Gap on the evening of 23 January, and at dawn the next day they were on a flat road. 'There was a German column just waking up and we drove through,' said Sadler. 'We thought we would drive in that direction to get as far away from the road as possible.'

The terrain became more rugged as they approached the Jebel Tebaga and wadis (dry river beds) ran from the hills down towards the road. The men were tired, having driven through the night, so Stirling decided they would rest for the remainder of the day in one of the wadis.

Grateful for the respite, the men climbed out of their vehicles and into their sleeping bags. 'Our big mistake was that we weren't vigilant,' said Redington.

'We'd been driving the whole night and were tired. We laid up in a wadi and I remember putting my Smith and Wesson [revolver] by my side. We could see the Germans from the wadi.'

Despite the proximity of the Germans, no sentries had been posted, which made the task of the men of Fallschirmjaeger z.b.V 250 all the easier. This German paratroop force had been deployed to North Africa specifically to hunt down the British special forces, whose raids on key installations had been so damaging. One of its members, Sergeant Heinrich Fugner, recalled that a native scout had picked up the trail of the SAS the previous evening. Now they were within striking distance. 'We dismounted and searched the wadi,' said Fugner. 'Since it was the middle of the day, our search was easy.'

Redington's slumber was rudely shattered. 'Someone was kicking my feet and shouting "*Raus, Raus!*",' he recalled. 'I looked up, saw a German standing over me and reached for my Smith and Wesson. But it was gone.'

Stirling and his men had been caught napping and were captured, all except Sadler and two sergeants, Johnny Cooper and Freddie Taxis, a Frenchman, who had been asleep at the top of the wadi. They escaped by running out of the wadi and hiding among some desert scrub. Sadler recalled:

> 'Luckily we managed to get into a little narrow gully among the bushes. Then some goats came round us. There was a shepherd, but I don't know if he had seen us. We didn't make ourselves known, we just laid doggo [in concealment]. We stayed there till dark and in the meantime they took the rest away along with the jeeps. We heard them move off.'

Stirling's war was over. He was captured at a pivotal moment in the evolution of the SAS. For the Allies, the North African campaign was reaching a triumphant denouement, and the question of what the future held for Britain's special forces – or 'private armies', as they were called in some quarters – had been a subject of discussion for several weeks at Combined Operations HQ in London.

David Stirling had his faults; the obstinacy of which Brigadier Davy spoke was one, but his determination and charisma had been vital in establishing the SAS as a valued fighting force in North Africa. Without him, could the SAS survive whatever lay ahead?

Chapter One

The entry in the 1SAS war diary on 14 February ran: 'Lt-Col A.D Stirling, D.S.O (Scots Guards), the Commanding Officer of this unit, was officially reported as missing, believed prisoner of war. Major Mayne returned from Syria.'

Paddy Mayne had left Egypt for the Ski School in the Lebanon (the French Mandate of Syria included present-day Lebanon) on 24 January – coincidentally, the day that Stirling was captured – along with six officers and seventy-seven other ranks from A Squadron.

They had returned from operations in Libya in early January and been posted to the Ski School to learn the skill in anticipation of a future deployment to the Balkans.

Stirling's capture had thrown all future plans into turmoil. The day after Mayne reached Kabrit, on 15 February, so did Major Earl George Jellicoe, who returned from operations in Libya upon learning of Stirling's misfortune. The pair arrived to encounter, in the words of a fellow SAS officer, Captain John Lodwick, 'chaos'. He continued: 'A great and powerful organization had been built up, but it had been an organization controlled and directed by a single man; Stirling alone knew where everybody was, what they were doing and what he subsequently intended them to do.'

A caretaker CO had been appointed, Major Vivian Street, but he had only joined the regiment in the autumn and was rather keen to return to his parent regiment, the Devonshires, which he had joined in 1932. He explained this to Lieutenant Colonel Bill Stirling, who descended on Kabrit in the middle of February to assess the scale of the 'chaos'.

Bill Stirling had been appointed commanding officer of No62 Commando in October 1942, and for many weeks had been party to the consultations about

Bill Stirling joined SOE early in the war and left the organisation to take command of No62 Commando in 1942.

the future of British special forces. Lieutenant General Dwight Eisenhower, Supreme Commander of the Allied Expeditionary Force of the North African Theatre of Operations, admired what the SAS had accomplished in North Africa and wished for a similar force to be deployed for operations in the Western Mediterranean. Bill Stirling was selected to command the force on 2 February 1943 and flew to Algiers, location of the Allied Force Headquarters (AFHQ). Not long after his arrival, Bill learned of his brother's capture, and Combined Operations HQ (COHQ) instructed Stirling to visit Kabrit and report his findings.

When he was back in Algiers on 28 February, Bill Stirling wrote a letter to Brigadier Bob Laycock at COHQ:

> 'There is no doubt that all SAS activities for the Mediterranean should be under one hand. I am having a shot at it myself but I am handicapped by lack of status and the fact that SAS has asked that I be appointed to command them as well as the party here … . I do not think it matters in the least who commands SAS so long as it is someone who has this idea and who controls small raiding

activities so far as personnel is concerned over the whole Mediterranean basin.'

On 9 March, the SAS war diary recorded: 'Lt Col H.J Cator, MC, assumes command of the Regt.'.

Henry – he preferred 'Harry' – Cator was a 46-year-old decorated veteran of the First World War, a former member of the 2nd Dragoons (Royal Scots Greys). In January 1940, Cator had

Paddy Mayne was a pre-war rugby international who believed in the principles of self- disciple and physical fitness.

volunteered to command a new unit called the Auxiliary Military Pioneer Corps, which subsequently became No51 Commando, and he had a reputation for quiet, efficient managership. He was not a gung-ho, lead-from-the-front CO, but more a discerning chairman of the board, wise and temperate, able to delegate. His full title was Commanding Officer, Raiding Forces, and he received his job description on 8 March:

'You will have under your command:-

'a) New SAS Commando Squadron
'b) New SAS Small-Scale Raiding Squadron
'c) Greek Squadron (Sacred Heart)
'd) Raiding Forces Signals
'e) Light Repair Section
'f) Any other forces that may from time to time be put under your command.

'You will not command in operations. Units or sub-units will normally be put under comd [*sic*] of a local commander for operations.'

It was explained to Cator that his responsibilities would primarily be training, administration and discipline. On the other hand, he would not be 'responsible

Like Paddy Mayne, Bill Fraser joined the SAS from No11 Commando and was an audacious special forces officer.

for detailed planning or carrying out of operations'.

The appointment of Lieutenant Colonel Cator as CO of the Raiding Forces led to a swift reorganization of the units under his command. On 19 March, the 1SAS war diary stated that the regiment had been 'reorganized'. D Squadron had been designated the Special Boat Squadron (SBS) under the command of Major Jellicoe, and 1SAS had been renamed the Special Raiding Squadron (SRS) with Major Paddy Mayne in charge. The diarist added: 'Various officers and men who the new establishment is unable to cater for have been warned for other jobs or units'.

In effect, Mayne used the reorganization as an opportunity to cull the regiment of those soldiers whom he regarded as unsuited to special forces soldiering. Several were upper-class officers who had been recruited by David Stirling and were regarded by Mayne as being temperamentally unsuited to irregular warfare.

Lieutenant Colonel Cator proved an astute commander, adhering to his responsibilities and refraining from intervening as his units began training for the war in Europe. 'As far as Raiding Forces Headquarters were concerned, they might just as well have not existed for all the effect they had on our training or our control,' reflected Lieutenant Peter Davis, who had joined 1SAS in December 1942. 'All decisions rested solely with Paddy.'

Mayne divided his force of approximately 280 men into three troops. Number 1 Troop was under the command of Bill Fraser, along with Mayne the only surviving officer of the seven who had joined L Detachment in the summer of 1941; Major Harry Poat was OC of 2 Troop and Captain David Barnby was in charge of 3 Troop – he was later replaced by Captain Eric ('Ted') Lepine.

'For the first month every man in the regiment had to go through a second recruits' training,' remembered Lieutenant Davis, 'and pass a test in all elementary subjects based on the standard TOE tests [Table of Organization and

Tony Marsh, left, and Harry Poat, third from left, joined the SAS in the winter of 1942/3 and were instrumental in the regiment's evolution.

Equipment] before carrying on with the more advanced and more interesting training.'

The training was carried out at the SRS's base at Azzib in Palestine (modern Achziv), the culmination being a timed route march in which those who failed to pass would be Returned to Unit (RTU'd), a fear that haunted them all. The route was from Tiberias, on the western edge of the Sea of Galilee, which was 600ft below sea level, to the camp at Azzib, a distance of approximately 45 miles.

Private Sid Payne recalled:

'We had 24 hours to do this march but it was across desert and over hills and back down again. I'd just had a pair of boots repaired and they were perfect, well broken in and comfortable, so I wore them. By the time I finished they'd completely split and the bottom was all away from the top. I think my Troop did the march in 23 hours but it was terrible.'

Paddy Mayne trained his men relentlessly at their Palestine camp throughout the spring of 1943.

As well as the physical training there was more specialized instruction, which was devised and overseen by Mayne. Men were schooled in the use of American and Axis weapons, light and heavy machine guns, and a mortar section of one officer and twenty-eight other ranks was established. There were night exercises on the coastline from landing craft, as well as instruction in cliff-scaling, wire-cutting and map-reading.

Each of the three troops was divided into two equal sub-sections, each under a corporal or lance sergeant. These sub-sections were further subdivided into three-man squads of specialists: Bren gunners, riflemen and rifle bombers. In addition, each troop was assigned a mortar section, engineers' section and signallers' section.

Peter Davis was impressed with Mayne's organization: 'Each sub-section was, on paper at least, a highly efficient little fighting unit, capable of providing its own support in many of the usual situations which one expects to meet in battle.'

Mayne was weeding out the weak – physically and mentally – from his regiment so that only the most suitable men remained. By the start of May, the training began to ease off and there were opportunities for more recreational pursuits. 'The SRS held a sports meeting at Azzib,' recorded the war diary on 2 May. The SBS and Raiding Forces HQ sent teams, as did the New Zealand

2nd Division Officers Training Cadet Unit (OCTU). 'OCTU won with the SBS obtaining second place,' noted the SRS diarist. 'The meeting was a great success. The New Zealanders providing plenty of beer. The tote made a profit of £17 out of which a shield is being made for the winning team.'

One of the rare successes for the SRS on the sports day was the rugby seven-a-side competition; the fact they had in their team Paddy Mayne, who had played rugby union for Ireland and the British Lions before the war, had given them a distinct advantage.

The SRS helped themselves to their share of the plentiful beer provided by the generous New Zealanders, and Mayne, who had a reputation as a binge drinker, had worked up a particular thirst on the rugby field. Sid Payne remembered:

'It was very hot and there were six of us in the tent, trying to stay cool. The captain came rushing through and he said "Out, quick, Paddy's looking for someone to booze with". So we all shot out the tent. He was like that, looking for someone to booze with. He was a hard drinker and he expected everyone to be the same.'

Mayne was an intimidating character. He was physically imposing, standing at 6ft 2in and weighing 15 stone, but his manner and the way he bore himself was also disconcerting to the men under his command. Lieutenant Peter Davis recalled 'his piercing blue eyes [that] looked discomfortingly at me, betraying his remarkable talent of being able to sum a person up within a minute of meeting him'.

Davis expected a voice and a character to match the powerful physique, but quite the contrary:

'I was struck by the incongruity of his voice and of his shy manner. His voice was low and halting, with a musical singsong quality and the faintest tinge of an Irish brogue. I was soon to learn that when he was excited or intoxicated, this remarkable voice would become so Irish as to be hardly intelligible, and when he was angry it would reach such heights as to be almost a falsetto.'

Few of the soldiers knew Mayne as well as Lieutenant Mike Sadler, who had operated alongside the Irishman in both the LRDG (Long Range Desert Group, a reconnaissance and raiding unit established in Egypt in 1940) and the SAS. Sadler reflected:

> 'Paddy felt his true vocation in war. He was well suited to war and he enjoyed it. He was very good at fighting the Germans but he was also a solicitor and a very able sort of chap. But he wasn't totally fearless; there's this slight impression around that he wasn't at all scared. He was well aware of the risks around at any particular moment, and I don't think he fancied the idea of being shot more than anyone else. But he had a very good control of himself.'

Chapter Two

While Bill Stirling had been in Egypt, assessing the extent of the disorder caused by the capture of David Stirling, the rest of No62 Commando had been on a ship headed to Algiers. It was a small unit, numbering just forty-nine men, including Bill Stirling, with Major Geoffrey Appleyard his second-in-command. Among the other seven officers were a Scot, Captain Roy Bridgeman-Evans, an American, Lieutenant John Cochrane, and a Frenchman, Lieutenant Raymond Couraud. The latter was known on the troopship as Raymond Lee, a former French Legionnaire and a veteran of the St Nazaire raid of 1942; what Lee kept hidden from his comrades was his activity between deserting from the Legion after the fall of France in June 1940 and arriving in England a year later. Lee had absconded from the Legion in Marseille in the south of France, where he remained, becoming entangled in the city's underworld. He fell in with some mobsters and was part of a lucrative smuggling enterprise, but when he fell out with the boss over a woman, Lee fled France and made his way to England via Spain.

Cochrane was from Buffalo in New York, and the outbreak of war in 1939 coincided with his graduation from university. He ventured to Canada in the autumn of 1939 and was commissioned into the Toronto Scottish Regiment. Seeking more adventure, Cochrane volunteered for No62 Commando in November 1942, outlining his motivation in a letter to his parents on January 5 1943: 'Without having any sort of hero complex I did want to see some action and being in the Commandos seemed to me to be the best way of getting it.'

Cochrane found his fellow commando officers 'an awfully nice bunch of lads', and he characterized Geoffrey Appleyard as 'a naturally born leader and I for one would follow him anywhere'.

Two other officers had gone ahead of the rest of the Commando, instructed by Bill Stirling to fly to Egypt and liaise with Lieutenant Colonel Henry Cator

Major Geoffrey Appleyard was the second-in-command of 2SAS and brought his vast experience as a commando officer to bear during training.

and Majors Paddy Mayne and George Jellicoe about future raiding operations in the Mediterranean. The pair were Captain Philip Pinckney and a Dane, Lieutenant Anders Lassen. Both had distinguished themselves on operations with No62 Commando the previous year, and Pinckney in particular was a popular figure among the men. Known as PHP (his middle name was Hugh), Pinckney was a product of Eton and Cambridge, but despite his privileged background he had no airs or graces. He had spent much of the late 1930s on the road, exploring Egypt, India and Tibet. Upon his return to London, he worked for a tea importers, and when the war came it was an opportunity for the 6ft 3in Pinckney to once more spread his wings. 'He was not one for bullshit,' remembered one of his men, Sergeant Horace Stokes. 'He allowed us to wear what we needed to wear according to what we were doing. This was of course completely at odds with how the "normal" army operated and sometimes it didn't win friends with senior officers.'

Pinckney's culinary tastes were equally unorthodox, and he derived great satisfaction from what Mother Nature provided. A fellow SAS officer, John Lodwick, recalled that Pinckney 'would spend hours in the fields collecting

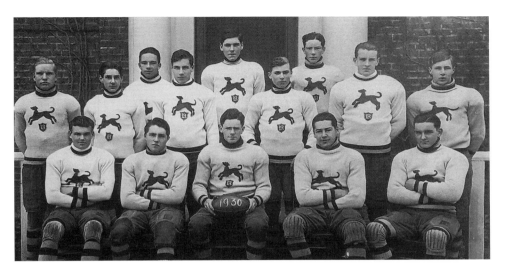

John Cochrane, seen here in the front row second from left, was an American who joined the Canadian army in 1939 and later volunteered for the commandos and later 2SAS.

snails, slugs, grasshoppers and other apparently inedible faunae'. He would also harvest dandelions and nettles and out of them make a giant salad, one his men were obliged to taste.

Stokes was good friends with Sergeant Tim Robinson, the pair being early volunteers for the commandos and seasoned guerrilla fighters by the time No62 Commando docked in Algiers on 4 March. Untested as a combat soldier was another NCO, Corporal Robert Lodge, who, like Raymond Lee was serving under a *nom de guerre*. His real name was Rudolf Friedlaender, and at 34 he was the oldest man in No62 Commando. Lodge was actually a German Jew who had left his native Berlin in 1933, shortly before he was due to sit his final law exams. His experience transformed him into an ardent socialist, even though he came from an upper middle class family, and having settled in England he retrained as a carpenter because he preferred living among the working class. He got engaged to a young woman, Win Lodge, adopting her name when he enlisted in the British Army in 1940, having secured naturalization as a British subject.

From the dock they boarded some 15cwt trucks and headed to Constantine, and from there to the coastal town of Philippeville (modern Skikda), 300 miles east of Algiers and 100 miles west of the Tunisian border.

A ruthless and daring commando, Anders Lassen (foreground) was a Dane who was sent to North Africa by Bill Stirling on a fact-finding mission in early 1943.

No62 Commando established their camp among the sand dunes about 10 miles east of Philippeville, their tents surrounded by wild lavender. Appleyard told his parents it was 'a most delightful place ... wonderful surfing and great fun with the boats for training in surf work, etc, and the length and height of the surf is about Newquay standard'.

One of the results of Philip Pinckney and Anders Lassen's visit to Kabrit in February was the acquisition of a couple of 1SAS sergeants to help in the training of No62 Commando. One was David Leigh, an Australian, and the other was a popular Liverpudlian, Dave Kershaw, known as 'Honest Dave' on account of his bookmaking skills. 'They had been sent to give us the benefit of their experience, and they certainly did,' said Horace Stokes.

Bill Stirling trained his men hard in the spring of 1943. Three years earlier, he had been the driving force behind the establishment in Lochailort, north-west Scotland, of the Special Training Centre, unofficially known as the School of Guerrilla Warfare, where throughout the summer and autumn of

1940 hundreds of new commandos came to be instructed in stalking, navigation, unarmed combat, climbing, amphibious landings and demolitions. Stirling had been the chief instructor (brother David had been among the first intake of pupils in June 1940) and he now imparted many of this skills to the men of No62 Commando.

At the end of March 1943, Appleyard wrote to his parents. He started with a description of his appearance: five days' growth of beard on his face, no clothes on his body, sitting on a rock in the middle of a stream with his feet in the water, bringing relief to his blisters. 'This is quite the toughest thing physically I have ever done,' he continued. 'We are each carrying 65lb packs ... this country is most incredibly difficult to move over and through, and the maps are abominable so that one mile per hour is quite a good average speed.'

Captain Philip Pinckney, left, was an unorthodox man who found his niche in the irregular warfare of the commandos and then 2SAS.

While his men were put through their paces, Bill Stirling shuttled between their base at Philippeville and Algiers, headquarters of the AFHQ for operations in the Western Mediterranean.

The war in North Africa was nearing its climax – at the end of March, the Eighth Army broke through the Mareth Line in southern Tunisia, precipitating the withdrawal north of the Axis forces and their eventual surrender on 13 May – and Stirling was instructed to write an appreciation of how No62 Commando might assist in the forthcoming invasion of Sicily.

Stirling submitted his three-page document on 29 April. He began by explaining why the SAS could be so effective, a clear indication that Stirling was already in the throes of forming a second SAS regiment:

'SAS Regt, after initial training by parachute, operates in such numbers as are most suitable for the task in hand, and is specially trained to gain access by any means available. A loose organization by squadron, Tp [troop] section and group makes it possible to operate without notice or reorganization in small or large numbers. SAS troops will normally be employed where vital tasks exist which cannot conveniently be tackled by regular formations, and more particularly which lie far behind the enemy lines.'

The transition from No62 Commando to the Second Special Air Service Regiment (2SAS) officially occurred on 13 May 1943. There was no fanfare to the birth of a sister regiment to 1SAS, but Bill Stirling was authorized to expand his unit.

In the middle of May, Major Appleyard was instructed by Stirling to fly over the Italian islands of Lampedusa and Pantelleria, situated in the Mediterranean between the east coast of Tunisia and Sicily, and take some reconnaissance photographs.

One of the photographs revealed a radar station on Lampedusa, 75 miles east of Tunisia, and Stirling chose this as the site of the inaugural raid of 2SAS. The men selected for the operation practised canoeing in the two-man folboats (made from wood and canvas) and cliff-scaling before they were briefed on the mission.

The SAS were led to believe by AFHQ intelligence that there would be scant opposition, with the main garrison on the island stationed several miles east of the landing beach on the western tip of Lampedusa. This intelligence proved to be faulty. One of the SAS raiding party was Robert Lodge, who wrote in his diary:

'We paddled with utter care, the little whirlpools of phosphorus sparks seemed to light up our boat. We looked forward awaiting the signal from the scouts, but we neared the cliffs and no sign. We touched the rocks with our paddles, but as no signal came we had to turn right to skirt the shore.'

As the SAS paddled around one of the cliffs, they came under fire and the order was given to withdraw to the Motor Torpedo Boat (MTB) out to sea. Lodge continued:

'A searchlight suddenly sprang up out of the darkness to our left, sweeping across the water. Our first thought was a patrol boat, perhaps an E Boat. That would have been the end. We had about a mile to get back to the MTB, which could not move nearer for fear of being caught in the searchlight.'

It required nearly an hour of hard paddling before they reached the safety of the MTB, exhausted but relieved.

The Pantelleria operation, codenamed *Snapdragon*, was launched on 28 May, its purpose being to seize a prisoner for interrogation from among the 13,000-strong Italian garrison. The eight SAS soldiers, commanded by Major Appleyard, were transported to within half a mile of the island in the submarine *Unshaken*. They paddled ashore in two RAF rescue dinghies, painted black for camouflage instead of their normal yellow. 'The whole plan was calculated to a split second – so many minutes to get ashore, so many minutes for the raid, and so many minutes for the return to the submarine,' recalled Lieutenant John Cochrane, in charge of one of the two dinghies.

The SAS landed without incident, said Cochrane, who continued:

'[A]fter posting one sentry on the two dinghies Geoff [Appleyard] started off in search of the way up that he had already seen from the submarine – no mean feat in the pitch blackness. We had one false start and then began the hardest climb any of us had ever experienced – and we pulled ourselves up completely by instinct and every foothold was an insecure one, the rock being volcanic and very porous, crumbling away under our hands and feet.'

Once they had scaled the cliff, Appleyard, Sergeants David Leigh and Horace Stokes and Lance Corporal Ernie Herstell moved inland through thick gorse bushes in search of a sentry. They soon encountered one, but as Appleyard leapt on him, the Italian emitted a strangled cry. It was heard by other sentries, and in the subsequent confused fire-fight Ernie Herstell was shot. Cochrane, waiting on the cliff top with his section, saw Appleyard tearing through the gorse, followed by Leigh and Stokes. They descended the cliff in record time – about a minute and half in Cochrane's recollection – with the only casualty being a nasty injury to Leigh's knee.

Sergeant David Leigh, seen here at his wedding in 1944, was chosen by Paddy Mayne to assist 2SAS as a training instructor in the summer of 1943. He was later commissioned and was killed in action three months after his wedding.

'Somehow or other we all managed to find the boats and started to paddle like mad for the rendezvous with *Unshaken*, which was lying submerged offshore,' said Cochrane. The pre-arranged pick-up signal with the submarine was the detonation of two grenades in the sea, and the explosions swiftly brough the *Unshaken* to the surface. 'What a relief it was to see her!' Cochrane added. 'We clambered on board and down the conning tower in double quick time, while hefty sailors slit the rubber boats in little pieces and sank them.'

The third and final 2SAS operation of May 1943 was codenamed *Marigold*. Its target was Sardinia and the aim was the same as the ill-fated Pantelleria raid: the capture of a prisoner for interrogation in the hope of filling in some gaps in Allied intelligence prior to the invasion of Sicily, Operation *Husky*.

Unfortunately, the outcome was similar to what had unfolded on Pantelleria. The eight-strong raiding party, commanded by 23-year-old Captain Pat

Dudgeon, paddled ashore from the submarine *Safari* against a heavy swell. Inadequate intelligence about the landing beach meant that the SAS had to then overcome a terrain of loose shale that further slowed their progress. Exhausted, one man dropped his weapon as he struggled uphill. 'I can still hear the clatter now, it seemed to echo round the beach,' Private Harold 'Tanky' Challenor recalled years later. 'In seconds a machine gun and a rifleman opened up in our direction. Then the enemy lit a ground flare and suddenly, from pitch darkness, it was Piccadilly with the lights on.'

Not the for the first time, the 2SAS raiding party withdrew, or as Horace Stokes put it 'headed back to Philippeville with our tails between our legs'. Not that he was dispirited. 'Sometimes things just went completely wrong, not just a bit wrong,' he reflected. 'I remember thinking … it would be a miracle if any of us were going to make it through the war.'

Lieutenant Anthony Greville-Bell, who had taken part in the aborted attack on the radar station at Lampedusa, was also philosophical about the setbacks:

'You don't seethe against anyone. It's funny, you just laugh about it and say what a bloody balls-up; you get so used to it in the British army, or any army. The thing about war is that you plan and plan but the ones that win are the ones who are most able to overcome disasters, because nothing ever goes the way it's supposed to.'

Chapter Three

On Thursday, 13 May, General Miles Dempsey, commander of XIII Corps, visited the SRS at Azzib and watched the squadron undertake a night exercise. He stayed the evening, and the next morning Dempsey gave a lecture in the camp cinema on security. The squadron then went on leave until Sunday morning, Major Paddy Mayne following after he had lunched with Dempsey at Raiding Forces HQ.

The rest of the month was one of hard work, a continuance of the training they had been subjected to throughout the spring. On 25 May, a mortar platoon arrived at the camp, comprising one sergeant, a corporal and twenty-three other ranks. It was placed under the command of Captain Alex Muirhead. 'Alex had never handled a mortar before,' remembered Lieutenant Peter Davis, 'but this ignorance on his part was put to good effect, for by training his section entirely along his own ideas, and in complete defiance of the training manual, he was able as a result of this conscientious experimenting to mount the mortar and fire the first round accurately within 20 seconds.' There was the odd mishap along the way, however, such as the occasion when, through a miscalculation, Muirhead inadvertently directed five bombs rapid-fire straight down under his own observation post, which was sited about a quarter of a mile beyond the actual mortar position. Muirhead emerged from the salvo with a wry grin on his dusty face, his only wound a small cut on the back of his head from a sliver of shrapnel.

On 5 June, the SRS war diary noted, they were preparing 'to move to an unknown destination'. They departed Azzib the next day at 0530 hours. The 'unknown destination' was Suez, where for nearly three weeks they practised amphibious landings from LCAs (Landing Craft, Assault) in the Gulf of Aqaba and rehearsed neutralizing a cliff-top gun battery; they knew the real thing was imminent, and they guessed it would be somewhere on Sicily, but the exact

Bill Fraser, Derrick Harrison and Alex Muirhead, pictured in 1943, all led their men with aplomb during operations in Sicily.

objective remained a mystery. They had accurate sketch-maps of the objective, recalled Davis, 'every detail of which was to be learned thoroughly by each man in the unit. Routes to be taken, not only by each section, but also by other sections and other troops were studied and memorized.'

The only omission was place names, to the extent that the SRS didn't even know in which country lay their objective. By late June, however, every man in the squadron knew meticulously the plan of attack: 1 and 2 Troops would land by LCA on the south coast of a peninsula approximately 400 yards from the target – a battery consisting of four coastal guns, to the west of which were a group of garrison huts, presumably living quarters. These huts were to be captured by 1 Troop in a frontal assault; 2 Troop would in the meantime swing round to the west and attack the gun battery from the northern (inland) side. The role of 3 Troop, which would land half a mile west of the other two troops, would be to seize two farms located on high ground about 600 metres inland. A road between the farms and the gun battery was the only one on the

The Combined Operation Assault Pilotage, seen training here, was a naval special forces unit that reconnoitred Cape Murro di Porco prior to the SAS assault.

peninsula, described by Lieutenant Davis as 'a toe'. In fact, the actual location of the SRS objective was a 'nose': Capo Murro di Porco, the Cape of the Pig's Snout, which lay in the south-east corner of Sicily.

The objective had been reconnoitred on 9 June by Ralph Stanbury, who belonged to a recently formed naval special forces unit called Combined Operation Assault Pilotage Parties – more commonly known as COPP. Their speciality was coastal reconnaissance ahead of amphibious operations, and Stanbury had been transported to the Capo Murro di Porco by the submarine *Unrivalled*.

While surveying the coastline through the submarine's periscope, Stanbury observed the lighthouse at the southern end of the cape, underneath which were steep cliffs. Then he spotted 'something squat and sinister just to the north of the lighthouse'. As Stanbury squinted through the periscope site, he realized it was a gun battery, one of four which commanded a wide arc of fire.

General Bernard Montgomery addresses Paddy Mayne and his on board the Ulster Monarch shortly before the Cape Murro di Porco operation.

It looked an impregnable position, until the submarine headed a mile west. Stanbury recalled:

> 'At the base of the peninsula, on the south side, where it jutted out into the sea, there was a narrow rock beach formed by a sudden receding of the cliff. Behind it the ground sloped less sharply to the top of the peninsula, and there were clumps of trees and small bushes which would give cover to troops after they landed. It seemed quite conceivable for a small band of Commandos to land in this place and to make their way down the peninsula for a mile to the battery.'

Eighth Army commander General Bernard Montgomery inspected the SRS at Port Said in Egypt on 28 June on the deck of the *Ulster Monarch*, a former passenger ferry converted into a troopship that was capable of carrying six LCAs and 580 soldiers. Launched in Belfast in 1929, the *Ulster Monarch* was 359ft in length and had a crew of 130.

Sid Payne remembered that Mayne introduced Montgomery to Graham Rose, the Regimental Sergeant Major, but Monty ignored him: 'So Paddy grabbed hold of Monty and said "And this is my RSM!".'

Derrick Harrison's Two Troop section in Sicily 1943. Sid Payne is 2 from left b-row and Bob McDougall is 3 from left front-row.

There was further confusion when the SRS refrained from giving the general the customary cheer until he had reboarded his launch prior to visiting the next troopship. Montgomery dithered, uncertain if he should depart without the traditional hurrah. Peter Davis looked on as Monty took his leave of the *Ulster Monarch* muttering to himself, 'Wonderful discipline, wonderful discipline! Very smart. I like their hats.'

The SRS were then given a couple of days' leave. Most spent it in Cairo, having a final knees-up in one of the city's many bars, but for Paddy Mayne one evening got out of hand.

The exact circumstances of his fracas with Lieutenant Colonel N.G.F. Dunne, Provost Marshal of Cairo, are unclear. Mayne had probably drunk too much, making the most of one night when he was unburdened by the responsibility of command, and at some point he came to the attention of Dunne, of the Royal Irish Hussars. Dunne's nickname was 'Punch', suggesting he was also a feisty character who might have relished the chance to tame the legendary Mayne. The upshot was the arrest of Mayne, landing Lieutenant

Colonel Henry Cator with an awkward dilemma. He went to see his superior, Brigadier George Davy, Director of Military Operations in Cairo, who in turn went to see Brigadier John Crystall, in charge of security for the Cairo area. Davy recounted what happened next:

> 'He was an old friend of mine from before the war, a 13/18th Hussar. I went straight round to him and gave him all the facts and he agreed at once that we must let Mayne go. So he had him up for a few words of advice (which I should think could be quite forceful) and let him go. I was sorry to have to do this, because John had a hard job to keep discipline in his vast and largely moving population. Harry [Cator] then brought the contrite Paddy into my office to apologize to me for causing so much trouble. I thought that a bit unfair and turned the interview into a good laugh.'

The SAS sailed from Port Said on 4 July. Once at sea, Mayne briefed his men on the actual target, as laid down on Instruction No2, issued by XIII Corps:

> 'The task of your Sqn is to destroy the Coast Defence Battery.
> 'Time of Landing – H Hour
>
> 'On Completion of your task your Sqn will either:
>
> 'a) Rejoin *Ulster Monarch* direct (For this purpose you will make arrangements to summon the craft to the beach or other embarkation point selected by you), or
> 'b) Move Westwards to join 5 Div, who will be moving Northwards from Beach 44 towards Syracuse.
>
> 'The method to be adopted is left to your discretion on the spot, the object being to get your Sqn on board *Ulster Monarch* as soon as possible, and re-organized for further seaborne operations.
> 'If, during your withdrawal, you make contact with other hostile batteries or defended localities you will, if the task in your judgement, is within the power of your Sqn, destroy them.
> 'Wireless silence will be observed until H hour.'

Photographed in 2023, these are the rocks on which most of the SRS landed, enabling them to move swiftly inland without the need to scale cliffs.

Once the briefing was over, the men withdrew and prepared for the assault. The strength of the SRS was nineteen officers and 268 other ranks. Peter Davis recalled:

> 'Each man was left to his own thoughts and his own fears [as we neared the Sicilian coast]. As we waited for the landing which was now so imminent, it was too easy to look at the group of faces we had come to know so well and to let the thought possess us that almost certainly there would be many we would never see again after the next few days had passed.'

The *Ulster Monarch* was guided towards the target by the submarine HMS *Unrivalled*, aboard which was Ralph Stanbury of COPP. The sub had arrived in its position at 2300 hours on 9 July and, upon surfacing, it began shining a

Alex Griffith, far left b-row, and Bob Lowson, 4ᵗʰ from left b-row, pictured with the Liverpool Scottish prior to joining the commandos and then 1SAS.

beacon light to the south half an hour later. 'The tension on the conning tower of the submarine grew as the minutes passed and still there was no sign of the convoy's arrival,' noted Stanbury. 'Suddenly, incredibly close, we heard the three blasts on a siren that signifies a ship putting her engines astern.' It was the *Ulster Monarch* accompanied by its destroyer escort.

Just after 0100 hours on 10 July, the three troops transferred from the *Ulster Monarch* to the LCAs, 40ft vessels capable of holding thirty-five soldiers. It was a hazardous procedure; the sea was running high and the men were carrying up to 80lb on their back, with their Mae West life preservers further restricting their movement.

The men lined up in the gangways in their allotted positions, the open loading bay hatches giving those in front a glimpse of the dark swell beyond. The LCAs were lowered on the davits down into the water on the port side. Sergeant Bill Deakins, in command of the Engineer Section, recalled that Major Mayne was one of the first to board an LCA: 'Each of us in turn, was helped by a matelot crewman who judged the swinging rise and fall as well as possible.' Once inside the LCAs, the soaked men lined up in three columns, two against the sides of the craft and one down the middle. The matelots then knocked out the

Geoff Caton (left), an SAS desert veteran, was the only fatality of the Cape Murro di Porco operation.

forward and aft davit hooks and the LCA was freed. 'Thankful to be underway for this unknown shore … the only noise was the low drone of the boat engines with the gurgle of the wash away from the sides of the craft,' added Deakins.

Many of the men were seasick, but as they neared the shore, the storm abated and the shouts of desperate men drifted on the wind through the darkness. They were British airborne troops bound for the Ponte Grande bridge, south of Syracuse, whose gliders had fallen well short of their target. Some LCA pilots refused to stop for the stranded paratroopers, insisting that they had to adhere to the timetable. Others did, including the LCA that contained Private Sid Payne of 2 Troop:

> 'We came across this wing of a glider and there were four of five men clinging to the wing. We took them on board. All their mates were dead. Whoever organized that [glider operation] should've been court-martialled because there was no way they could have landed safely. The terrain was all small fields and low walls, and the gliders were coming in, hitting the walls, tipping over and killing the blokes inside.'

Lieutenant Johnny Wiseman, a section commander in 1 Troop, also ordered the pilot of his LCA to collect whatever men they saw, one of whom was Brigadier

Philip Hicks, the commander of the airborne force. Wiseman recounted: 'I said to him "look, old boy, I can take you into the beach but you'll have to keep out of my line because I've got a job to do".'

Paddy Mayne's report on the Capo Murro operation was bald and shorn of any description of the short, sharp fight to neutralize the battery, known to the Italians as Lamba Doria. Having noted the time of the landing – at 0320 hours – he stated:

> 'No3 Troop attacked and captured Farm Damerio and mined and held the road. The 3" Mortar detachment engaged the battery position dropping their first bomb in the area 5 minutes after landing.
>
> 'No1 Troop made a frontal attack from the southwest, and No2 Troop made a left flanking movement, and attacked from the north.
>
> 'The position was captured at 0430 hours and the guns were destroyed at 0500 hours.'

Wiseman was tasked with leading the frontal assault on the battery's living quarters. Once ashore, he and his men moved towards the target as Captain Alex Muirhead's mortar section rained bombs on the Italian gunners. They snipped through the barbed wire undetected and waited for the mortar fire to cease. The moment it did, Wiseman struck, attacking the Italian positions with a swift ferocity. Wiseman, who was subsequently awarded a Military Cross for his courage and leadership, recalled: 'We landed, got up the cliff and the area where the gun had barbed wire round it and I got there first and we cut the wire. I thought it might be mined but it wasn't so we went through a gap I'd cut in the wire.'

The citation for Wiseman's MC described what happened next:

> 'Immediately the mortar fire finished he went straight in, achieving complete surprise, killing, capturing and wounding 40 of the enemy … although the darkness of the night made control difficult, he maintained complete command, and the information which he sent back was invaluable to the proper conduct of the operation.'

Like 1 Troop, the men in 2 Troop came ashore without difficulty; all the weeks of practising scaling cliffs had been a waste of time and effort. Sid Payne recalled that he wasn't scared:

> 'I think we took it in our stride. We had a good start because I never even got my feet wet as we came off the LCA and walked down the ramp on to the rocks. We had to climb the cliffs but that wasn't too hard. We got to the top with the barbed wire in front of us and the blokes assigned to cut the wire crawled forward and cut it.'

Peter Davis of 2 Troop also led his section to the top without impediment. While he made contact with Captain Harry Poat, Mayne's second-in-command, his men hugged the ground in defensive positions and listened to the explosion of mortar bombs from Captain Muirhead's section. The mortars were devastatingly accurate, one bomb landing in the battery's cordite dump. 'Muirhead and his mortar team were splendid,' remembered Corporal Bob Lowson. 'Before then I thought they couldn't fight their way out of a paper bag – most had come from some buckshee infantry regiment – but they were good.'

After the assault, Mayne presented Muirhead with a choice: 'Do you want a medal or a promotion?' Muirhead pondered for only a moment before replying: 'I'll take the promotion, Sir, my widow could do with some extra money.'

Having consulted Poat, Davis realized that they had come ashore half a mile further west than anticipated. This was because the captain of the *Ulster Monarch* had decided to sail closer to the shore than planned, meaning the pilots of the LCAs had their navigation thrown out.

Consequently, Davis's section was immediately below the battery, slap bang in the middle of what he knew to be the most dangerous area on the peninsula. Above the sound of mortar fire, Davis heard over to his left the 'very comfortable slow tat-tat-tat of a Bren ring out'.

The Brens belonged to 1 Troop, whose commander was Captain Bill Fraser, MC, one of the original SAS officers recruited by David Stirling in August 1941. On board the *Ulster Monarch*, Fraser had ragged 2 Troop that he would defy orders to attack just the living quarters, boasting: 'One Troop will wipe out the gun battery before 2 Troop even find out where it is!'

One of the coastal guns captured by the SRS on Cape Murro di Porco on the morning of July 10.

Because 2 Troop had been landed in the wrong place, the well-rehearsed assault plans were redundant. Furthermore, Davis was unable to find the rest of 2 Troop, so he improvised: 'Because we had landed so far from our intended position, I decided to take my section straight in across the stretch of open ground separating us from the battery which could now be clearly seen standing out against the flames [caused by the mortar shell landing in the cordite dump].'

Davis and his men scurried across the open ground and immediately came under fire. It was evident it came from their left. Davis shouted the password, 'Desert Rats', and a back came the response in a Mancunian accent, 'Kill the Italians'.

Meanwhile, another section from 2 Troop, commanded by Lieutenant Derrick Harrison, was also sizing up the situation in lieu of the wayward landing. 'There was only one thing to be done,' adjudged Harrison. 'Retrace our steps and carry on with the original plan.'

When Harrison led his men around the back of the battery, a machine gun began firing at them from their right flank. Sid Payne moved towards the position. As he approached, the two soldiers manning the gun jumped to their feet and surrendered. Payne continued his advance: 'I hadn't gone very far and there was a bunker, and a chappie came round the bunker. We had the password "Desert Rat", but before I could say it I recognized the blue shirt.[1] But he didn't and opened fire with a Bren gun.'

The man firing was John 'Ginger' Hodgkinson, a rugby league player of some repute who was half a foot taller than Payne, and his burst was fortunately high. Payne described what happened as their advance continued:

> 'Anyway we shouted the password and carried on and practically ran straight on top of an Italian machine gun. It was sandbagged and there was a nest of barbed wire around it and so there was no way I could get into it. But they both stood up with the arms up and there was nothing I could do about it really except shoot the one behind the gun. He fell over the gun and knocked it over and it was out of action. Whatever happened to the other Italian I don't know because I pushed on. It was mayhem. All you could hear was "Desert Rats", "Kill the Italians", "Mama Mia". Actually it was a slaughter, some of them were in bed.'

Sergeant Joe Schofield and Private Alex Griffiths were members of the same section in 3 Troop, whose task was to land half a mile west of the other two troops of the SRS and seize the two farmhouses. Griffiths remembered that there were high spirits among the men as they approached the Sicilian coastline: 'We were singing and shouting as we came in. We had the padre with us [Ronald Lunt, who had been posted to the SRS a few weeks earlier] who told us to shut up. We were all happy-go-lucky and thought that these Italians are going to be easy.'

---

1. The SAS wore blue-grey shirts rather than the usual khaki of the British Army.

Seen here facing the camera, Reg Seekings was an SAS Original from 1941 who earned a Military Medal on Cape Murro di Porco to go with the DCM he won in the desert.

The men's voices died as they prepared to land, and so did the engines of the LCAs as the shoreline loomed. 'The doors went down and we ran off, the centre line first, followed by the two side files,' recounted Schofield. 'Instead of a sandy beach we hit sharp coral and scrambled across until we reached the sand beyond.' Not a shot was fired as the troops streamed inland, each section to its designated task.

As 3 Troop advanced, they heard the first salvo from the mortar section to their right. Schofield's section made for one of the farmhouses, which they had been informed was an Italian strongpoint and communications HQ. Aerial reconnaissance photos indicated it was defended by three tanks.

The SRS moved silently through the scrubland, which sloped gently uphill, when suddenly up sprang an Italian. He was shot in the head and almost at once the scrub came alive with frightened Italians. 'They were making so much noise, begging for mercy, there was no chance of surprising the farmhouse now,' recalled Schofield. 'We surrounded and entered the farm and surrounding buildings, overcoming the low-grade Italian infantry who surrendered after the first shot was fired.'

There were no tanks – the SRS later learned that they had been withdrawn a few days earlier – and within minutes 3 Troop had secured the two farmhouses and were turning them into well-fortified defensive positions. Griffiths was upset by the death throes of an Italian, who had been shot in the storming of the farmhouse, evidently a civilian who lived in the building. 'All the family were all around him and it took a long time for him to die,' said Griffiths. 'He was dying in the farmhouse, and the women were making a hell of a lot of noise. But they blamed the Germans, they viewed us as friends.'

Half a mile east of the farm at the battery, the four gun emplacements had been silenced and the crews either killed or taken into captivity. Bob Lowson, a member of Lieutenant Davis's section, arrived at the battery after its capture and recalled the scene:

> 'By the time we got there all hell had broken loose. One of the other troops were already in the gun battery and they were running around lifting the lids on these underground shelters and lobbing grenades down … in the morning [at first light] when we looked in these underground shelters, there were women in them. The Italians had their women living in them. It was a case of "that's tough".'

The engineer section attached to the SRS was commanded by Sergeant Bill Deakins. There were three of them, the others being Corporal Roy Chappell and Lance Corporal Jock Bowman, and they carried their explosives in Italian mountaineering rucksacks.

'I'd been given a photo of the guns before the operation,' recounted Deakins, 'but they were nothing like the actual ones. These were British, manufactured at the end of the First World War.' Deakins and his section began to lay the charges on the guns. Suddenly two Italians appeared, eager to help in the demolition of the guns. Deakins was in no mood for interference: 'We had to literally kick these Italians out of the emplacements for we could not be sure this was not some sort of ploy or trick.' Deakins and his two engineer comrades continued with their work. 'We opened the breech and put a charge across the hinges. It was a five-second charge which gave us just enough time to sprint for cover.'

Deakins said there was a thunderous explosion and then a rain of twisted metal pattered down on the concrete base of the emplacements: 'I went up to Paddy [Mayne], saluted and said "Guns out of action, Sir".' At 0520 hours, Mayne fired the very light, the signal to the invasion fleet that the guns had been blown.

Lowson and his comrades sat down on the perimeter of the gun battery and looked south, where 'we watched this huge armada of ships'. They brewed up, satisfied with a job well done, and as they drank their tea they discussed how long it would be before they could get back on the *Ulster Monarch* for a proper breakfast. The only fatality of the operation had been Corporal Geoff Caton, a popular desert veteran, who had been shot as he advanced to take the surrender of a white flag. Caton was a member of Sergeant Reg Seeking's sub-section, and the devious manner of his death enraged the NCO. His response was brutal, described in the citation for the Military Medal that he was subsequently awarded: 'Seekings himself rushed the pill box and with grenades, and finally his revolver, killed the occupants. He then collected his Sub-section and advanced on and wiped out the mortar post, thus allowing his troop to continue their advance.'

As Lowson and the rest of 2 Troop watched the arrival of the main invasion fleet, their serenity was violently shattered. Suddenly, recounted Davis, 'we were roused by a sharp explosion from inland, which interrupted our peaceful reverie in the rudest way'. Several more great detonations followed, and out to sea, a short distance in front of the approaching invasion fleet, the SRS saw the water erupt. 'At once we realized that another coastal battery, a mile or two inland, had started to engage our shipping,' said Davis. This battery was designated AS 493 by the Italian coastal defenders, the 'AS' denoting the Augusta and Syracuse Fortified Zone.

Paddy Mayne had by this time established his HQ in one of the two farmhouses, Farm Damerio, seized by 3 Troop. He radioed 1 and 2 Troops and told them to rendezvous on his HQ. They arrived with dozens of Italians – soldiers and civilians – as well as several wounded British glider troops. 'With all the prisoners and released glider troops the squadron had difficulty assembling again in order of battle prior to advancing,' said Sergeant Schofield. The answer was simple: Mayne ordered the glider troops to guard the Italians, and at 0800 hours he issued instructions to his men.

Number 2 Troop were instructed to lead the assault, supported by 3 Troop on their left flank and 1 Troop on their right. Harry Poat ordered Derrick Harrison's section to be in the vanguard of the attack.

Harrrison's section moved north-east from the farmhouse, advancing across fields that offered little in the way of protection except, here and there, a poorly constructed stone wall. The fields extended to a line of trees, beyond which they heard the boom of guns. Private Sid Payne recalled:

> 'We used those same walls for cover as we moved across and a very funny thing happened. We'd got across this field and we moved towards this farm when we noticed there were tomatoes in this field. So we sat behind the wall and left the rifles poking over the top of the wall.'

Harrison's sergeant, James McDiarmid, a hard-bitten Scot who had joined the SAS a year earlier, detected a sniper among the trees. 'We were down behind our own little wall slinging shots at the tin hat,' said Harrison. 'Then we were over and after him.' The sniper withdrew further into the copse, but a grenade eventually brought him out with his hands up. Harrison stripped him of his rifle and ordered him to walk to the farmhouse, an instruction the Italian was only too willing to obey.

To his left, Harrison heard the chatter of a Bren gun as 3 Troop encountered resistance from an orchard. Private Harry 'Ginty' Hill, a Welshman who had only joined the SRS a few weeks earlier, was shot in the neck.[2] 'The enemy, seen lying on platforms in the trees, were quickly dealt with,' said Joe Schofield. 'Others found in camouflaged foxholes were also overcome without much difficulty.'

Those Italians who did not surrender withdrew through the trees to the coastal battery. Meanwhile, Harrison had radioed HQ to ask for assistance and Peter Davis was ordered to move up his section in support. On arriving, Lieutenant Davis found McDiarmid 'in full control of the situation and throwing 36 grenades in all directions, although no Italian was to be seen'.

---

2. Hill recovered from his wound and rejoined the SAS, but in July 1944 he was one of thirty-one men executed by the Nazis behind enemy lines in Occupied France during Operation *Bulbasket*.

Davis, deciding to push on towards the battery, soon spotted three 'tubby green forms' among some olive trees. He gave them a burst with his Tommy gun but missed the target. Nonetheless, the Italians decided to give themselves up and were disarmed and sent south-west to the farmhouse.

Harrison's section was now under fire from a building hidden among some trees to their left. They returned fire from a dirt track as orders were shouted to prepare to storm the building. Suddenly, a white handkerchief was waved from one of the windows. The men inside were British glider troops who had landed a few hours earlier; they had taken the SRS for Italians because of their khaki drill trousers and blue-grey shirts, and only the sound of Harrison's instructions had alerted the gliders troops to their real identity. 'They began coming down with their hands up and I walked to them and said, "carry on, keep going", and a chappie at the back suddenly said "Hello Sid". I got the shock of my life. These were some of the South Staffs,[3] with whom I'd first joined the army.'

There was little respite for Harrison's section. Having directed the glider troops towards the HQ, he and his men were once more targeted from a farmhouse to their left. It wasn't on the route to the battery but Harrison decided it must be eliminated; ordering Sergeant McDiarmid and nine men to continue to the battery, he led the rest of his section (nine men) towards the farmhouse. Harrison took up the story:

> 'We had advanced not more than twenty or thirty yards when the firing stopped and seven figures stood up. They were about a hundred and fifty yards away and, although they had not got their hands up, none of them carried weapons. Holding our fire we advanced in open formation across the dry, sun-scorched fields. We were about thirty yards away from them when, without warning, they dropped from sight behind a concealed bank.'

At the same moment, a light machine gun opened up on Harrison and his men from the flank. The gunner was only 100 yards distant from the SRS but his aim

---

3. The 2nd Battalion of the South Staffordshire Regiment were the leading glider assault troops for Operation *Ladbroke,* the airborne assault to capture key ports and bridges near the Sicilian invasion beaches.

was not good. Harrison yelled at his men to withdraw to some broken ground a few yards to their rear, and to cover their manoeuvre he hurled two grenades towards the machine-gun position. Harrison and his signaller crouched down behind a bank just as his first grenade exploded. Then to their horror they saw an Italian grenade land a few feet from where they were. It was, remembered Harrison, a 'money-box grenade … but succeeded only in blowing us off our feet'.

The Italian grenade, also nicknamed a 'Red Devil', was the SRCM Mod. 35, coloured red and in Harrison's eyes resembling a money box. They had a reputation for ineffectiveness.

Harrison pulled out his German signalling pistol and fired at the Italians. His intention was to alert another SRS section to the enemy's position, but the signal cartridge he fired was 'successful in a way I had not dreamed'. It landed in the long dry grass close to where the Italian machine-gun nest was situated, and within seconds, aided by the gentle sea breeze, the grass was ablaze. The Italians withdrew into a cottage, at which Harrison fired three more cartridges. As smoke billowed from the building, he and his men broke cover and ran to catch up with the rest of their troop.

In their recollection of the attack on the second battery, Davis and Harrison recalled rendezvousing at a small white church; what stuck in their minds was the priest, who in English thanked them for sparing his church. Inside were huddled some locals – women, children and old men. Harrison remembered this incident as coming later in the day, after the batteries had been destroyed, but Davis said it was preliminary to storming the second battery. He recalled that they checked inside the church to make sure there were no soldiers hiding among the congregation, and then continued towards the target.

Battery AS493 was unusual in that it was deployed against enemy aircraft and shipping. Situated on one of the rare bits of elevated ground on Capo Murro di Porco, the battery's rangefinder was housed in a turret on top of an earthen mound.

Alex Muirhead's mortars were by now subjecting the position to a heavy pounding. One of the Italian officers operating the battery noted: 'The gun pit of No.5 gun took a direct hit from a mortar bomb. Another fell near the fire control centre. Some men were wounded, and others killed. We began firing with an 8mm machine gun, but soon this position also took a direct hit.'

As petrified as the Italians were, it was for the SRS a 'light-hearted affair' with the men realizing they were up against a poorly trained and ill-disciplined enemy whose heart was not in the fight. Davis recalled:

> 'After a time the lads began to take this situation for granted, and would deliberately expose themselves in order to draw the fire of the panic-stricken Italians, and thereby to learn their exact position. Nonchalantly chewing pieces of grass, or sucking at the small orange tomatoes growing in profusion all around, our sections pressed forward.'

Nevertheless, the climax to the skirmish was not so light-hearted. Under a creeping mortar barrage, the SRS advanced before charging the battery, which consisted of anti-aircraft guns. 'As we went in an Italian mortar team, crouching in their emplacement, fell to our bayonets,' said Harrison. Later, when the British sifted through the detritus of the Italians' arms and equipment, they discovered that although their opponents had been issued with mortars they had not received any bombs.

Sergeant Bill Deakins and his engineers were instructed to demolish the guns but they didn't have enough explosives to destroy them. 'To make the guns more than difficult to use, the traversing, elevating gear was badly damaged, leaving the guns almost swinging vertically,' he recounted. 'If the guns could be fired at all, the shells would be fired straight up into the air.'

Across Capo Murro di Porco were strewn several wrecked Horsa gliders and the corpses of some of the nearly 2,000 men who had taken part in the airborne assault. According to Sergeant Joe Schofield, a large stash of food was found in one of the bunkers of the anti-aircraft battery, and this was opened with its contents used to feed the many prisoners and airborne stragglers who had attached themselves to the SRS.

Number 2 Troop sat in the sunshine and looked north, where across the bay they could see Syracuse. Harrison recalled that someone suggested turning the guns on the town, but 'we were in the dark as to the position of our own troops'. Instead, Bill Deakins and his engineer section destroyed the guns.

It was now around midday, and the SRS sought shade from the blazing sun beneath the walnut and olive trees close to the battery. They sent out some of their prisoners on a tomato hunt and they soon returned laden with them, along with nuts they had gathered from the countryside.

Major Mayne recalled his men to his command post at Damerio farm, and for the first time the different sections and troops began to get a clearer picture of the morning's events. Davis was relieved to learn they had suffered only one fatality (Caton) and one seriously wounded (Hill), along with three men with minor wounds. One of the lightly wounded was Private Alexander Skinner, who had been wounded by fragments from a grenade in the first hour of the landing on Capo Murro di Porco. 'Nevertheless, he took his full share in the advance and continued to fight throughout the action,' explained the citation for his Military Medal. 'During the attack on the farm house Marse Aleona, he himself stalked and killed three enemy snipers.' Skinner dressed his own wounds rather than risk being withdrawn by the medics. Only three days later did he reveal the extent of his wounds, and he was evacuated to hospital.

Mayne totted up the result of the operation, and included it in his report:

> 'The following enemy guns were captured or destroyed:
> '7 C.D. [Coastal Defence] Guns 6 inch calibre
> '1 A.A. [Anti Aircraft] Gun 40mm
> '5 A.A. Guns 75 or 80mm
> '5 Light A.A. Guns 20mm
> '4 4inch Mortars
> '3 Range Finders
> 'MGs and LMGs [Machine guns and light machine guns]
> '500 prisoners were taken and 200 of the enemy were estimated killed or wounded.'

Mayne also noted that, to his chagrin, the squadron had lost one beret and three Bren gun magazines.

The SRS spent the afternoon mopping up the very small and isolated pockets of resistance towards the western coast of Capo Murro di Porco. Most of the Italians they encountered were waiting to be captured. Private Alex Griffiths recalled that a couple were even sitting on their suitcases, as if they were waiting for a boat to take them on a holiday cruise. All the prisoners joined a column that by late afternoon was a couple of hundred yards in length. It was guarded by just one soldier. 'In the course of their march towards regimental headquarters, the guard's magazine, which had not been properly inserted, fell out, leaving him blissfully holding a useless weapon,' said Davis. 'He only noticed his loss when a grinning Italian came running up to him and returned his magazine.'

By evening, the SRS had not made contact with the British 5th Division, as they had expected to do. They were now in a gentle valley which ran towards the main coastal road to Syracuse, and they decided to camp here for the night. The peacefulness of the evening was shattered by a barrage of anti-aircraft guns from some of the British ships at anchor off the coast. Lieutenant Peter Davis was one of several SRS men who looked skywards. There was a flight of twelve aircraft, identified by one soldier as German JU88s, intent on bombing the Allied shipping. 'As they progressed,' said Davis, 'from out of the clear sky there suddenly swooped about half a dozen Spitfires, which immediately engaged the attacking bombers with the speed and fury discernible even to us, in our position of ground spectators.'

Davis counted five JU88s shot out of the sky, to whoops of delight from the SRS, and the rest broke off their attack. Once that excitement was over, the men brewed up and a well was found to allow them to wash off twelve hours of accumulated dirt, dust and grease. It had been a long day, and a successful one, and who knew what tomorrow would bring. 'For warmth we pulled bundles of hay from the fields and snuggled down,' said Derrick Harrison.

Chapter Four

The Special Raiding Squadron remained on Capo Murro di Porco throughout the day of 11 July, enjoying the sun and the peninsula's tomatoes. The squadron's medical officer, Captain Phil Gunn, was so distressed by the emaciated children he saw that he organized among the men a collection of what they could spare from their rations and this stash was distributed among the youngsters.

Meanwhile, Major Paddy Mayne was receiving his orders from 5th Division about the next operation for the SRS.

Early on the morning of 12 July, the squadron marched down the dusty road that led to Syracuse. A minesweeper ferried the men from the harbour to their troopship, the *Ulster Monarch*, and they came aboard in high spirits.

Sergeant Bill Deakins, in command of the Engineer Section, described the rush for 'shaves, showers, sort out and clean kit, a more than welcome meal, change of underclothing'. He also said they received a message of congratulations 'from the top brass' – presumably General Miles Dempsey, commanding XIII Corps – and also one from Paddy Mayne. But he tempered his praise with an admonishment: 'If the squadron used as much ammunition in future operations, we would be sent to shore with five rounds apiece.' Deakins considered the threat justified. 'It is surprising how much confidence can be gained by firing off a few rounds, even if they have not the least hope of hitting a target. Perhaps an instinct to make sure the weapon is in good order.'

Lieutenant Peter Davis recalled that they had been back on the ship only a couple of hours before he and the other officers from 2 Troop were summoned to the cabin of Major Harry Poat, Mayne's second-in-command. On his bunk, surrounded by maps, looking as nonchalant as ever, he told the officers:

Some of SRS take a well-earned rest during the advance through Augusta towards the German positions to the south of the port.

'Take a map each of you, and find a seat somewhere. As you have probably heard, they want us to do another landing this evening. I know that the men are tired and need a rest, and how you all feel about another operation at so short notice, but they consider it important, and anyhow, it does not seem to offer many difficulties.'

Poat drew the officers' attention to their maps and pointed at what Davis considered a 'strangely shaped little peninsula'. It was, explained Poat, an important naval port called Augusta. Built on a spit of land attached to the mainland by a bridge, the centrepiece of Augusta was its vast brick citadel – actually a thirteenth-century castle with walls that were 2.5 metres thick – that commanded imposing views of the port and surrounding countryside. Intelligence reports stated that a white flag had been seen from the citadel and it was the task of the SRS to go ashore and ensure that the port was safe for a large-scale landing.

Poat explained that the assault would be in two waves: 3 Troop would be in the van, followed by 1 Troop, with 2 Troop in reserve. 'We must hold the town

Bill and Alf Dignum, seen here in 1942, were signallers who served in the SBS and SAS respectively.

against any counter-attack,' said Poat. 'And, if possible, will push forward to this T-junction, about a mile to the north of the town, which we will hold until the main forces reach us. They will not be many miles away and should make contact with us before dawn tomorrow.'

Poat made the operation sound routine, particularly as the white flag suggested the town had already capitulated, and it would be little more than a holding operation until the arrival of 17 Brigade of the 5th Division.

The only slight concern was that the landing would be made that evening at dusk. Poat dismissed the officers with instructions to brief their men. 'I do not think any of us fancied breaking the news to the men,' said Harrison. They had already guessed something was afoot when the officers were ordered to report to Poat. All Davis, Harrison and the other officers had to do was confirm their fears. Private Sid Payne remembered:

'Most of us were asleep and looking forward to a decent meal but we were woken up, then given a briefing, and told we had to attack Augusta. There was no grouching or grumbling. The only thing that did bother us was we were going to miss a meal. The sailors had got the meal all laid out, trays of bacons, eggs and sausages.'

Number 3 Troop were more apprehensive. They would lead the assault and their instructions, recalled Sergeant Joe Schofield, were to 'proceed straight through the town, cross the bridge and capture the railway station'. Once the station was secure, 3 Troop would advance down the track to a road junction about one-and–a-half miles north of Augusta. Here they would remain until contact was established with 17 Brigade.

The *Ulster Monarch* sailed from Syracuse in the late afternoon of 12 July. Sea conditions were perfect. 'Everything was calm and peaceful,' noted Schofield. 'Having completed our preparations we could only wait and enjoy the view.'

Escorted by the naval destroyers *Kanaris*, *Nubian* and *Tetcott*, the *Ulster Monarch* encountered the cruiser HMS *Mauritius* as it closed on Augusta. Davis was later told that the conversation between the two captains ran along the following lines:

'Mauritius:	*Ulster Monarch*, what the hell are you doing here?
'Monarch:	I am about to land troops in Augusta.
'Mauritius:	Advise against carrying out operations. Enemy strength unknown.
'Monarch:	I intend carrying out my orders and landing troops in Augusta as planned.
'Mauritius:	In that case, is there anything we can do to help?
'Monarch:	Yes. Follow along and support us if and when necessary.'

The skipper of the *Mauritius* also informed the *Ulster Monarch* that he had on board Rear Admiral Thomas Troubridge, Flag Officer Commanding Overseas Assault Forces, who had been heading to Augusta earlier in the day on HMS *Eskimo* when the ship came under fire from batteries located in the hills overlooking Augusta. Nineteen sailors were killed, twenty-two wounded and the *Eskimo* sustained severe structural damage.

According to Sergeant Schofield, the *Ulster Monarch* found the boom to Augusta open and the 'intrepid captain decided to enter and in we went'. They were now so close to the port that the soldiers got a good glimpse of their objective. 'The sight was amazing, white-painted houses surrounded the

Augusta looking north from where the SRS came ashore in the evening of July 12 1943. The Germans were situated on the high ground.

bay in which we now proceeded towards,' said Schofield. 'Seaplanes close in shore bobbed up and down on the gentle waves, ships were at anchor and by the dockside. All was very quiet and peaceful.'

The engines of the *Ulster Monarch* slowed and the soldiers heard the command, 'SRS Embark'.

Signaller David Danger remembered that as they sailed north, the SRS were offered Benzedrine pills, what the men called 'stay awake pills'. 'We were told they would give us some verve,' he said. 'It was an entirely voluntary thing. Some boys took them but I didn't because I've never liked taking pills or any form of medication.'

On the ridge overlooking Augusta to the north were the German troops of the Hermann Goering Division. They observed the first wave of SRS soldiers transferring from the *Ulster Monarch* to the LCAs. As the first shells began to fall into the sea the *Ulster Monarch* and the *Tetcott* both retaliated. The captain of the *Tetcott*, Lieutenant Commander Richard Rycroft, described his vessel's role in his official report on the landing:

'At 19:25 *Ulster Monarch* lowered her assault craft and a light high velocity gun opened fire from the ridge overlooking Augusta. It gave its position away by the smoke and I opened fire with 4-inch which quickly silenced it. There was also some machine-gun fire from some cement works near the shore and I proceeded to close as near as prudent – about three cables [a unit of length approximately 600ft] – and blasted the place with 4-inch, pom-pom and Oerlikon. The effect was terrific, especially as first HMS *Kanaris* and later HMS *Nubian* joined in. One gun however went on firing for some minutes, shifting his fire from the assault craft to the ships, but he hit nothing. I also searched some vineyards with 4-inch to discourage any enemy who might still be lurking in them. A two-gun light howitzer battery also opened fire, apparently with no spotting or organized control. He did no damage but I was quite unable to spot where it was firing from.'

'We could hear rounds thudding into the landing craft and the whoosh of shells exploding in the water all around,' said Lance Corporal Albert Youngman of 3 Troop, who was in one of the LCAs as they neared Augusta. Joe Schofield estimated that the LCAs were 300 yards from shore when the first enemy shell landed.

Back on the *Ulster Monarch*, Captain Derrick Harrison and Lieutenant Peter Davis watched from the upper deck, fascinated by the artillery exchange between the Germans on the ridge and the Royal Navy. The guns of HMS *Mauritius* roared and Harrison saw on the high ground in the distance small clouds of white as the shells exploded. The German guns continued to fire, though their ranging was poor and the shells went over the ships.

The gun crew of the *Ulster Monarch*'s 12-pdr concentrated their fire on some of the buildings on the shoreline, while the ship's four 20mm Oerlikon cannons pumped tracer shells at the same targets in streams of red.

One of the Royal Navy destroyers sped towards shore at full steam with all guns blazing. 'She was asking to be blown right out of the water but she kept

Sergeants Ernest Goldsmith and Bert Youngman, seen here in Brussels in 1944, were members of 3 Troop in the SRS.

right on, gun still firing until she was close inshore,' said Harrison. The vessel turned broadside-on to the battery, then steamed away and prepared to make another attack.

The men of 2 Troop watched as the LCAs carrying 1 and 3 Troops dropped their doors. 'We couldn't get in because it was too rocky,' recalled Signaller Alf Dignum, 'so the Navy chap says "Sorry, you'll have to swim for it". I had the radio on my back and I didn't want to get that wet.'

The soldiers waded through the water, their weapons held above their heads, aware of the incoming fire from inland. Once out of the water, they had to negotiate a jumble of large smooth, slippery boulders.

Stretcher bearer George Shaw was fatally hit as he tended a wounded man. 'He was bending over a colleague when all of a sudden he collapsed to the ground,' said Dignum. 'I just got out of the way quick and hoped I wasn't next. Having a wireless strapped to you back doesn't exactly help matters.'

On the *Ulster Monarch*, the voice of the First Officer was heard on the loudspeaker above the din of battle: 'SRS, Second wave, standby to embark, port side only.'

The men of 2 Troop hurried below decks. On their way to the LCAs they passed the kitchen, and Sid Payne and some of the other soldiers pilfered what they could. 'I grabbed a handful of sausages and I was eating them as we climbed into the LCAs,' said Payne.

The soldiers embarked swiftly and silently. At the front of the LCA containing Davis and his troop, Private Bill Stalker was positioned behind the twin Vickers medium machine gun ready to engage the enemy as they closed on the landing area. Close to Stalker was his good friend and fellow Merseysider Bob Lowson. 'We weren't happy at having to land in daylight,' said Lowson. 'Somebody thought it a good idea, but we didn't.'

Stalker fired a burst at the waterfront, and a second later Davis felt a gentle bump and then the doors of the LCA flew open:

> 'We find ourselves leaping into about two feet of water. As we stumbled over the slippery rocks, bullets chip into the ground around us and someone from the previous wave yells at us to get into single file and out of the beach area which is under heavy fire from the machine guns across the bay. Bent low, we double through a small gap to find ourselves in a narrow street, sheltered temporarily at least, from the watching eyes across the water.'

As Captain Harrison and his section came ashore, they saw two bodies, those of Shaw and Corporal John Bentley, also a medic, shot dead as they tended to their comrades in the first wave. Captain Phil Gunn, the medical officer, was crouched over the pair, collecting their personal effects.

Harrison led his men along the same route taken by Davis, through a succession of small narrow backstreets of houses that at least gave them protection from the Germans on the ridge, although Sid Payne, a member of Harrison's section, said they still came under fire:

> 'There was still sniper fire in the town and we got to a position a bit further in and myself and Taffy Pitman were lying with the Bren. I was behind it and he was lying alongside me. Then all of a sudden there was a ping and it hit the wall above my head. Then another ping and this time the bullet hit the barrel of the gun. I didn't wait for the next one as I knew we were being targeted and knew we were being bracketed. We rolled out the way and took better cover. I think the only reason I survived that was because it was starting to get dark.'

Davis had split his section in half as they padded down the streets in their rubber-soled boots, one sub-section on each side, watching the doors and windows opposite. 'Proceeding slowly thus, we eventually reach a wider thoroughfare,' said Davis. This was the Via Principe Umberto, normally bustling with shoppers and diners, but not a soul was to be seen this evening. 'It is a tense business,' continued Davis. 'In the eerie half-light, we jump at every shadow, expecting to meet opposition from each corner, from every doorway. By now a ghostly silence pervades the whole scene.'

Sergeant Bill Deakins and his engineers had landed in the second wave. Unlike Capo Murro di Porco, where their skills had been required to blow the coastal guns, the engineers at Augusta were serving as infantrymen, nervously clutching their .30 American carbines. Number 3 Troop had to fight its way up the Via Principe Umberto. 'Broken doors and window frames, some caused by our advance in an effort to cut off or circumnavigate defence positions, were widespread,' said Deakins. Shop windows were broken and glass littered the pavements.

From further inland, 2 Troop heard a burst from a machine gun. Davis and his men froze before continuing their slow, cautious advance, scanning the balconies of the houses above them, grander and more elegant than those where they came ashore. No one was seen; the shutters were firmly closed. At the top of the Via Principe Umberto, they came to a large public garden, a popular meeting place in more peaceful times. Paddy Mayne had established his command post at the southern edge of the garden, but

Some of the SRS photographed at the corner of Via Cristoforo Colombo and Via Epicarmo as they advanced north through Augusta.

he had gone forward with 3 Troop and Harry Poat was the officer issuing instructions. Poat ordered Davis to make a sweep of the garden in the rapidly fading light, and having ensured it was clear of the enemy, to join up with Harrison's section at a large air-raid shelter on the eastern edge of the garden.

It was dark when Davis rendezvoused with Harrison. The men made themselves comfortable and waited. 'Intermittently, the silence of the night is shattered by a furious burst of machine-gun fire or the sharp crump of bursting mortar bombs,' recalled Davis. 'There is fighting somewhere ahead.'

It was 3 Troop fighting. Having come ashore under heavy fire, they had enjoyed a temporary respite as they trotted through the narrow side streets that led to the Via Principe Umberto. Once on the main thoroughfare, however, the trouble really began. The first to be hit was Sergeant Doug Eccles, who

The same location today.

was shot in the leg. 'Blood everywhere,' remembered his pal, Corporal Arthur Thompson. 'You didn't want to leave your mates, but it was instilled into you: keep going and finish the job no matter what. So I told him help was coming and pressed on.'

Then Sergeant Andy Frame was shot in the shoulder, just below the neck. With both medics dead, he dressed the wound himself and continued. 'We advanced down the street dodging from doorway to doorway,' said Sergeant Joe Schofield. At the top of the Via Principe Umberto, 3 Troop crossed the public garden, overshadowed by the vast, dark, austere citadel. No firing came from its walls. A road sloped down from the garden towards a bridge that linked the old part of Augusta to the newer area. It was now dusk, recalled Schofield, and once over the bridge 3 Troop divided into its two sections and headed for their objectives. Number 3 Troop was commanded by Captain Ted Lepine and its two section leaders were Lieutenants John Tonkin and Michael Gurmin. According to Schofield, 'at this time a section officer went missing'. It was Gurmin, so Lepine took over his section.[4]

---

4. Gurmin had joined the SAS in 1942, volunteering from the Middle East Commando. He left the SRS three weeks after the Augusta operation.

One section advanced either side of the railway line, the other moving forward along the road that ran parallel to the track to the east. Tonkin's section went down the road, but before they reached the crossroads they came under German mortar and machine-gun fire. Captain Alex Muirhead's mortar team were called up over the radio, and he directed three high-explosive and three smoke bombs on the German positions. His notebook recorded the results: 'Nil. Out of range.' Faced with superior firepower, 3 Troop took up defensive positions and waited. A runner was sent back into the town across the bridge.

Captain Lepine had led his section along the railway line in the same direction as Tonkin's. One of the men in the section was Lance Corporal Albert Youngman, who described what happened next: 'Out of the darkness on the other side of the wall came a patrol of Germans. We filed past each other. We weren't sure who they were and neither were they. They got about 20 yards past us before we let go with the Bren gun and got them. I walked over to make sure they were dead and picked up a Schmeisser [MP40 machine pistol] and a Luger … . I used the Schmeisser for the rest of Italy.'

Lepine's section rendezvoused with Tonkin's just south of the crossroads, where they positioned their men in an outer defensive ring, waiting for the German counter-attack they believed was imminent. 'It was obvious to us the enemy were there in force,' reflected Schofield. 'Fire came towards us on fixed lines, tracers ricocheting off the buildings and down the streets. The enemy were making a lot of noise and mechanical vehicles could be heard. We waited and held our fire.'

One of the 'mechanical vehicles' advanced towards the SRS. As the panzer emerged from the darkness, 3 Troop fired a PIAT anti-tank shell. The projectile glanced off the tank and exploded in the road behind, but the tank withdrew.

Further down the road at the railway station, the telephone rang in the stationmaster's office. A sub-section had been positioned at the station and one of the SRS picked up the receiver. Three minutes later, the enemy thus alerted to their presence, shells began to crash in and around the station. Alf Dignum, one of 3 Troop's signallers, tried to contact the Royal Navy warships in the harbour, but the radios had been damaged by sea water during the landings.

The Germans attempted to outflank the SRS on their left but they were spotted and driven back. 'Some enemy fell, the rest ran away,' said Schofield.

Once Augusta had been secured the SRS threw a party, which included a sing-song round a piano in the public garden.

'The enemy wounded were crying out but there was nothing we could do for them.'

Paddy Mayne was now at the station, weighing up the options. With no radio contact, no sign of 17 Brigade and only half the normal complement of ammunition – the operation had been launched at such short notice that the SRS had not had time to replenish the ammunition they had expended at Capo Murro di Porco – Mayne decided that before dawn broke the most prudent course of action was to withdraw to the public garden on the high ground overlooking the bridge.

He sent a runner to inform Harry Poat of his decision, instructing him to use 1 and 2 Troops to form a strong defensive position around the citadel, ready for the expected German armoured counter-attack. Davis positioned his twenty-four men among the turrets and archways of the citadel, which to him resembled a cross between a fortress and a monastery.

Harrison's section was also in the citadel, alongside Muirhead's mortar section. 'We settled down to wait, a cold night in front of us and one which we knew we might never see if the enemy attacked in strength,' reflected Harrison.

Taken in 2022, this photo shows the bridge over which the SAS advanced in Augusta from the direction of the citadel, visible in the background.

For several hours, the men of the SRS strained their eyes and ears for the enemy, but the darkness revealed nothing. 'Suddenly, at about four in the morning, we sat up with a jerk,' recalled Davis. 'Again we caught the faint sound – tanks moving along the road. The noise reached us in waves, sometimes loud and sometimes almost inaudible according to the vagaries of the mind.'

For a moment he feared the worst. Then the sentry in Davis's section ran over and excitedly told him that the tanks belonged to 17 Brigade. Furthermore, the lead tanks in the column had already reached the crossroads, discovering that the Germans had withdrawn during the night.

Mayne moved among his men, praising them for their conduct during a difficult and uncertain operation in which two of their number had been killed and six wounded.

Mayne also wrote a memo of gratitude for the fine work of Lieutenant E.C.S. Pratt, RNVR, who had commanded the LCA flotilla that had transported the SRS to their objectives at Capo Murro di Porco and Augusta:

'During the training he and his crews worked extremely hard and were always willing to take us out and to practise. His boats were kept cleaner and more workmanlike than any other flotilla I have worked with or seen. There was never a case of any mechanical breakdown. For the Murro di Porco Operation he had the difficult job of putting us down on a very rocky beach, which he did, in my opinion, perfectly. There was no confusion, no hurry, no noise.

'On the Augusta raid the LCAs were engaged as they were approaching the beach and as they beached. Lieutenant Pratt was the first ashore and held his LCA steady while we were disembarking. Although still under fire he waited around and re-embarked our wounded. I would very much like to have him and his flotilla for any future operation we may do.'

But for the time being, all thought of future operations was the last thing on the minds of Mayne and his men. 'The town was now ours, and the Squadron Commander set us free,' said Schofield. 'There was a dash for the shops and bars, mainly for vino.'

It was a party for the officers as well as the men. 'We spent the remainder of that day until late in the afternoon wandering around the town, entering any building we chose, and making deep inroads into the town's alcoholic beverages,' recalled Peter Davis.

When the infantrymen of 17 Brigade began marching through Augusta, the SRS festivities were well underway. 'I went into one bar and there was one of our officers holding a bottle of champagne,' recalled Sid Payne. 'He said "Come and have a drink", and knocked the top off the bottle on a table and we had a drink together.'

Derrick Harrison's overriding concern was to fill his stomach. Once he had accomplished that task, he wandered down to where they had come ashore and sat on the same boulders he had clambered over in fear just twelve hours earlier. The sea was calm, the sun warming up, and there wasn't a ship to be seen as he looked south.

By the time Harrison got back to the public garden, the party was in full swing: 'Someone had dragged a piano out of a cafe onto the sidewalk and a sing-song was in progress. The strain on our nerves released, everyone was now in high good humour.'

Two newsreel men chanced upon the scene, recording the festivities before downing their cameras and joining in the celebrations.

One of those enjoying the piano concerto in the public garden was Bill Deakins. Then a soldier appeared to tell him his presence was requested by Paddy Mayne in a bank. He arrived to find the massive Irishman standing before a large safe. 'Sergeant,' said Mayne to Deakins, 'I want you to open this safe.'

But how? Deakins had no explosives, so improvisation was the order of the day. 'I asked if about six hand grenades could be collected, some envelopes and a lot of string,' he recalled. Once he had these ingredients, Deakins removed the detonators and the powdered explosive from five grenades, and fashioned some sausage shaped charges using the envelopes and string. 'To fire the charge, I had kept back one complete grenade, [and] made sure that the mechanism was

John Tonkin, right in France in 1944, was a charismatic and bold officer in Three Troop.

working on the safety pin loose in the socket,' Deakins continued. 'I rearmed with the detonator fuse and wedged the grenade against the charges.' He then trailed a length of cord from the grenade detonator safety pin around the corner of the room to the staircase. Boom! Deakins's invention worked, but it was a crushing anti-climax for the safe contained mainly documents. There were six silver spoons tied in a bundle and a cameo brooch, which Mayne presented to Deakins as a token of his esteem. Deakins thought his mother would like the brooch.

By early afternoon, 17 Brigade were flooding into Augusta and their senior officers were not amused with the frivolity they encountered in the public garden. Even the squadron's padre, Ronnie Lunt, had entered into the spirit of the occasion, although he assured the men that the bottles of wine he was clutching were purely for the purposes of communion.

One 17 Brigade officer stormed over and demanded to know who was in command. The SRS men pointed to a giant figure 'pushing a pram along the street full of booze'. All complaints, they chortled, should be directed to Major Mayne.

Schofield remembered that it was around 1600 hours when the squadron was 'rounded up' and marched, somewhat inelegantly, towards the harbour. Waiting to transport them to two destroyers anchored offshore was an old motorboat. By nightfall they were back on board the *Ulster Monarch* in Syracuse harbour. Any hopes, however, that the SRS had for a peaceful night's sleep after the exertions of the past thirty-six hours were shattered by a German aerial attack. 'All that night we lay sweating in our bunks, with blankets over our heads in an effort to keep out the shattering roar of the heavy guns and the shuddering explosion of the bombs falling round us,' said Peter Davis.

They survived the onslaught, but the squadron's strained nerves were not helped the next day when they learned that another operation was imminent, this time against the well-fortified port of Catania.

Chapter Five

Despite the failures of the inaugural 2SAS operations against the islands of Lampedusa and Pantelleria, Lieutenant Colonel Bill Stirling remained positive that his regiment was headed in the right direction.

On 4 June, he had outlined a plan to Allied Force Headquarters for the deployment of 2SAS in the forthcoming invasion of Sicily. The strength of his force was at this time barely 100, but they were actively recruiting and this figure would rise steeply in the coming weeks. There were five operations in total: *Columbine*, *Gardenia*, *Forget-met-Not*, *Dandelion* and *Hollyhock*. By now, AFHQ understood that one of Stirling's little quirks was to codename 2SAS operations after his favourite flora, many of which he grew on his lavish estate at Keir in Scotland.

The five operations – involving ninety-six men in total – would all have the same purpose, namely to 'harass the enemy by attacking communications, roads, railways, signals and convoys by destroying power cables, harassing headquarters and reporting on

Philip Pinckney concealed a bad back in order to lead Operation Speedwell, but the consequences were fatal for the brave officer.

movements of enemy troops'. Eighty of the men would be landed by two submarines while a party of sixteen would insert by parachute. 'The potential value of this force should become greater when Catania has been captured and the enemy falls back,' explained Stirling, who added that his men would be resupplied by parachute. The 2SAS force would remain in the hills of north-east Sicily until they were able to join up with Eighth Army.

A detailed plan broke down the operational area of the five parties, their targets, their means of communications and how they would exfiltrate. Each party would carry sufficient arms, food and water for a minimum of ten days.

On 20 June, Bill Stirling was informed by 15th Army Group that Operation *Chestnut* – a mission to cut Axis lines of communication in northern Sicily in support of the Allied invasion – was cancelled. The next day, however, he heard that the cancellation was not definitive and that a conference to decide its fate would be held on 22 June, the upshot of which was a modified plan. Instead of insertion by submarine, 2SAS would parachute into their operation area in six transport aircraft; thereafter the plan was as initially envisaged. The reason for the cancellation of the original plan was the decision to use the two submarines on Operation *Hawthorn*, a Special Boat Squadron mission against the island of Sardinia.[5]

On 25 June, Major Geoff Appleyard wrote a letter to his parents, apologizing for his silence of late but blaming it on a very busy period:

> 'The unit is now really taking shape and I have considerably more responsibility than I have had before … my own personal command is now the equivalent of a company. I am entirely responsible for "A" squadron of 12 officers and 156 men, and am also, as Operations Officer, responsible to the Colonel for all the units operations – planning, laying on, and executing. And that involves 450 men. Bill Stirling is still in command of the regiment and I think we are building up something that will do great things

---

5. Operation *Hawthorn* was a costly failure, for two principal reasons: many of the SBS raiders succumbed to malaria, which was rife in the Philippeville area, and also the treachery of their Italian-American interpreter, whose allegiance turned out to be for the country of his ancestors.

in the future … . 2nd SAS stands for 2nd Special Air Service regiment and all ranks are now parachute trained, although that is by no means our only means of entry. I am personally more interested in the other way, as that is where all my own personal experience is. 2nd SAS is, of course, the brother regiment of 1st SAS – David Stirling's force, which did such great work in the Middle East.'

Appleyard wrote again on 7 July, once more having been very busy in the preceding few days. He had been making final preparations for Operation *Chestnut*, organizing or ironing out any logistical issues. He had been stood down from operations by Bill Stirling, who sensed that Appleyard was jaded and could benefit from a couple of months without the pressure of missions. Appleyard was honest enough to accept Stirling's decision, but had persuaded his CO to at least allow him to accompany the insertion party on the flight to Sicily. 'I go away from the camp again tomorrow, perhaps for two or three weeks, but should get mail forwarded at intervals,' wrote Appleyard to his parents. 'Dearest love. God bless, Geoffrey.'

Robert Lodge, who had contracted malaria shortly after returning from the raid on Lampedusa in May, rejoined the regiment in June to learn he had been promoted to sergeant. He recalled that they received confirmation of the Operation *Chestnut* on 11 July:

'The briefing we got about the operation was very complicated. We had it all in about half an hour, little time to digest it, far less to be able to learn codes for messages. We had to establish HQ and, all going well, to guide in the other planes on following days by wireless and then start operating behind the lines against the enemy's communications.'

The men on Operation *Chestnut* were split into two raiding parties of ten men each. One, codenamed *Pink*, was commanded by Captain Philip Pinckney, and the second, *Brig*, was led by Captain Pat Dudgeon. Lodge was in Dudgeon's stick, to his chagrin, as he was 'not on especially good terms with him'. Furthermore, all his friends were in Pinckney's party, an officer for whom Lodge had a more favourable opinion. That was a minor cavil, however; for

The Albemarle was a twin-engine transport aircraft from which the SAS parachuted into Italy.

Lodge, as for the rest of the men, 'this was the job we had always longed for and we were very keyed up'.

The day was spent drawing stores and special equipment, including their American overalls. Normally, an escape kit comprising money, a map on a silk handkerchief and a small compass would have been sewn into the lining of the overalls, but they hadn't the time to spare with a needle and thread so instead everything was stuffed into the pockets of the overalls. Their weapons, rations and explosives were stashed in their rucksacks. According to Lodge, they carried only .45 Colt revolvers.

At 2000 hours on 12 July, the twenty soldiers climbed into two Albemarle aircraft at Kairouan airbase in northern Tunisia. Major Appleyard was travelling as an observer with Pinckney's party, and also along for the ride with Appleyard was Major John Lander of the 21st Independent Parachute Company, members of which were attached to the *Chestnut* party as signallers.

Before Appleyard boarded the aircraft, he made a point of shaking the hand of every man involved in the operation. Lodge felt it was a 'great moment when we filed into the plane'.

The aircraft that contained the *Pink* stick was piloted by Wing Commander Peter May, a decorated and experienced airman of 296 Squadron. He took off first, followed ten minutes later by the Albemarle flown by Flight Lieutenant Smulley, inside which was Lodge, who later wrote:

> 'The aircraft banked a little, [and] the regular throbbing of the two powerful engines filled the air. Somehow I fell into a kind of half-stupor in the heat and the din, but we had to do the most important job yet: to hook ourselves onto the static line. This was to be done only on orders from a pilot after flying about half an hour. When the order came, we all helped each other checking the pins after the hook was placed. Somehow everybody looks two or three times at that vital connection. You know it is done and yet you must make sure over and over again. Then finally you relax, drop the line and forget it. Now darkness fell and the sea became only faintly visible … . I lost sense of time. I was leaning against the pneumatic door of the pilot and often, when he turned his seat a little, I awoke, feeling my 'chute move. My legs felt cramped and I was thirsty.'

The route was across the Mediterranean to Sicily, proceeding up the east coast of the island until they reached the ancient hilltop town of Taormina, whereupon they headed inland towards a DZ (drop zone) close to Randazzo, around 25 miles west. They came under fire from anti-aircraft batteries on Sicily, but any apprehension evaporated when they were told from the cockpit that they were ten minutes from the DZ. Lodge wrote:

> 'We get ready, fixing our crash helmets and adjusting straps. We know that we have to jump at the appearance of a green light, preceded by a red warning signal. But the men in the rear of the stick cannot see the lights and must therefore rely on the orders from a pilot or from a front of a stick. Suddenly, from the front, comes the cry, "green light, jump". We scramble forward, one

after the other disappears in the abyss, now the man in front of me drops through the hole, I fling myself forward and I'm caught by the slipstream.'

Dudgeon's stick dropped from a height of 2,500ft north of Sperlinga, approximately 40 miles south-west of Pinckney's DZ. The Albemarle from which they had jumped returned safely to Kairouan, but the second aircraft containing Geoff Appleyard and John Lander never arrived.

Early on 13 July, Vladimir Peniakoff[6] signalled Bill Stirling that Appleyard was missing, and he therefore had no knowledge of whether the *Pink* party had successfully inserted. Stirling, who had been at La Marsa in Tunisia, the HQ of the Mediterranean Air Command that was controlling all air operations against Sicily, flew to Kairouan and took over command of A Squadron.

Captain Pinckney's stick had indeed inserted, as described in his operational report:

'Dropped at 2330 hours onto hilltops of very steep volcanic rocks with some beech trees. Some of the party dropped no more than 300 feet. Difficult to collect stick and containers owing to rugged terrain. Nine of the party collected by dawn, and four containers found, emptied, and hidden … missing two containers found at dawn. One burst open due to thrown rigging lines, and two men's kit completely destroyed, including weapons, water bottles, rucksacks, sleeping bags, food, and one walkie-talkie. The other contained water which had all leaked away.'

Pinckney set up his command post under one of the beech trees, and not long after first light on 13 July he released his two pigeons, which flew off carrying messages strapped to their feet. He then assessed the situation. Two of his men had been injured on landing, including one of his signallers, Gibson, who had broken several ribs. One man was still missing – this soldier, Carter, trekked

---

6. Major Vladimir Peniakoff, from a family of Jewish Russian emigrees, was the founder and CO of a British special forces unit in North Africa called No1 Demolition Squad, unofficially known as Popski's Private Army. In July 1943, he was in Algeria and Tunisia training volunteers for the SAS and LRDG.

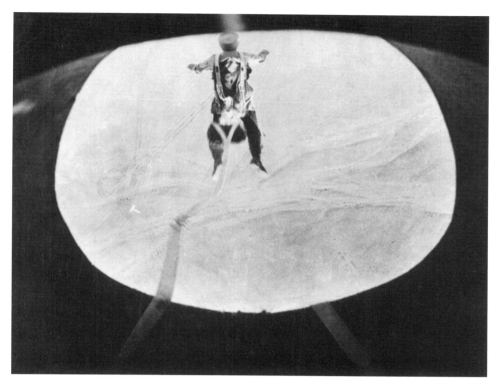

The SAS learned to parachute at their base at Kabrit, 80 miles east of Cairo, as seen in this photograph.

east on his own and eventually reached advancing US troops nine days later. Gibson was lucid enough to inspect the wireless equipment and report that the Eureka/Rebecca transponding radar was not working properly. Without it they would be unable to communicate with the aircraft expected that evening with a ten-strong reinforcement party

The Eureka part of the radar was a ground-operated transponder, which emitted a single morse letter continuously prior to the expected time of the aircraft's arrival. As the plane approached, the Rebecca transceiver and antenna system on board picked up the signal on its radar screen, enabling the pilot to identify the DZ.

The *Pink* party spent the day concealed on the hillside, resting their bruised bodies and hoping that the transponder could be fixed in time for the arrival of the reinforcements. But it wasn't, and although they heard aircraft above them shortly after midnight, no reinforcement stick dropped.

Captain Roy Bridgeman-Evans, second left in this photograph taken in Scotland in 1944, was a courageous and competent 2SAS officer.

Pinckney divided his party into two: he, Sergeant Bill Foster and Privates Kessel and Jones would head north and cut communications on the Messina–Palermo road, while Captain Robert 'Buck' MacDonald, a Canadian officer, and three men would perform a similar task on the Gangi–Palermo road that lay to the west. Signaller Gibson would remain at the command post with the wireless set.

It was 'extremely rough going' for Pinckney and his party as they moved north. The scrub was thick and impeded their progress, cutting and slashing their legs. They covered 25 miles in two days, skirting the village of Sant'Angelo on the evening of 18/19 July. They made a hideout in a small patch of scrub overlooking the coast road and railway that night, and the next morning they encountered a peasant. Pinckney addressed the Sicilian in German, but wasn't entirely convinced that the peasant fell for the ruse. They quickened their pace, and on the evening of 19/20 July they went to work.

'Laid 24hr time bombs at foot of one telegraph pole, and two double telephone poles,' wrote Pinckney in his report. 'Laid pressure switches and charges under railway line to derail the train across road. This took an hour, in which time one staff car, and four lorries, containing a few Italian soldiers passed.'

They retired south to a vantage point, and to the west spotted a train coming from the direction of Cefalù. The saboteurs rubbed their hands in glee, but their anticipation turned to disappointment when the train terminated at a station a mile from where the line had been mined. They did hear one explosion that evening, but they set out to their hilltop HQ unsure of whether it was the result of their handiwork.

Upon his return, Pinckney discovered that Gibson had at least got their walkie-talkies working, but that good news was offset by the stricken Captain MacDonald, who was suffering badly from malaria. Two more sheep were slaughtered for food that evening, 21 July, and on the next day the SAS party went off on another mission. With MacDonald still incapacitated, Bill

Geoffrey Appleyard, photographed pre-war, was an innovative and intelligent 2SAS officer whose premature death in July 1943 was a terrible blow to Bill Stirling.

Foster was nominated by Pinckney to lead the second sabotage party containing two men. Foster was from Workington in Cumbria, an artilleryman who had volunteered for the commandos upon their formation. He had been wounded during the Norwegian Vaagso raid of December 1941, survived the Dieppe raid the following year and was then transferred to Bill Stirling's No62 Commando in February 1943. There were few more experienced men in 2SAS.

Nevertheless, neither Foster's nor Pinckney's men had much joy in their attempts to harass and disrupt the enemy. Unbeknown to them, on 12 July Field Marshal Albert Kesselring, in charge of all Axis forces in the theatre as Commander-in-Chief South, had concluded that the west of Sicily was already lost because of Italian defeatism and that his best strategy was to use his German forces to defend the north and east of the island against the British advance.

Consequently, there was scarcely any enemy traffic to be seen heading in either direction along the east–west coast road. The first troops of any significant number that Sergeant Foster's party encountered were Americans advancing east on 24 July. Pinckney destroyed some telegraph poles, but the few Italians he encountered were deserters. On 27 July, he also made contact with the Americans and was driven to Palermo, liberated by the Americans five days earlier. In early August, Pinckney was reunited with Captain Pat Dudgeon, commander of Operation *Chestnut*'s *Brig* party.

They had dropped from 2,500ft – far too high – a result, Dudgeon learned later, of a malfunctioning despatch light that had turned green too early. Of the ten men who had jumped, Dudgeon was able to collect only three, and one of those, Private Gaspare, was feverish with malaria. Dudgeon had strained his knee on landing, which restricted his movement, and to compound their problems none of their containers could be located. These contained 30lb of plastic explosive, 30lb of ammonal, primers, detonators and fuses; in short, everything they needed to carry out their sabotage tasks. The containers also had rations, clothing, ammunition and medical kit.

They were able to muster between them one Sten gun with four full magazines and four Colt .45 automatics, each with two spare magazines. They each had one box of rations.

Nevertheless, Dudgeon remained upbeat. A reinforcement party was scheduled to drop the following night, but to Dudgeon's dismay it did not drop the men on the DZ and so he 'decided that the party must operate independently'.

Give their limited arsenal, Dudgeon recognized that all they could hope to achieve was to ambush some light transport. They observed the Nicosia–Cesaro road, but the traffic was too heavy in both directions and the cover too sparse. They instead cut some telephone lines.

Gaspare's malaria was worsening, but fortunately a farmer took them in and for a few days Dudgeon and his two fit men went out each day, gathering intelligence and cutting telephone wires, until they made contact with Canadian troops.

As for the six men who had become separated from Dudgeon upon jumping from the Albemarle aircraft on 12 July, they were experiencing adventures of their own. One, Signaller Alan Sharman, had landed without injury in a ravine but had been unable to make contact with the rest of the stick. He was captured three days later by the Italians and taken to Randazzo, where he was reunited with the other five members of the stick, among whom were Captain Roy Bridgeman-Evans and Sergeant Robert Lodge. Captivity for Lodge, a German Jew, was particularly dangerous. Fortunately, the Italian intelligence officer did not pick up on his heavily accented English during his interrogation. Lodge recalled:

> 'He mixed harmless with forbidding questions. When he noticed he could not trick me like that, he became menacing: stressing the point of uniform, he said the American overalls were not a recognized British uniform, etc. He carried on in that way, making me understand that I would be treated as a spy because of the uniform, the lack of a cap badge and the possession of a sum of Italian money. We had been well instructed to expect such attempts at intimidation, and I just repeated mechanically that, as a soldier, I could not say more than give rank, name and number.'

The prisoners were transported to the Sicilian port of Messina on 20 July, and the next day they were taken across the Messina Strait to the Italian mainland, together with an assortment of other British and American soldiers captured in recent days. The 2SAS men were all anxious to escape, particularly Lodge. Their opportunity came the next day when they were held in a railway station at Gioia Tauro prior to transportation to a POW camp in northern Italy.

That evening, Lodge, Bridgeman-Evans, the officer's batman, Private Mason, and Sharman slipped out of the station, easily evading the disinterested sentries. They headed south, sustained by fruit and vegetables that grew in abundance in the fields they crossed.

By dawn they were 10 miles south of Gioia Tauro, on a cliff overlooking a beach on which were a number of fishing boats being pushed out to sea for a morning's work, but also a sentry post. They agreed they would steal one of the boats the following night and sail it west, across the Messina Straits and then along the northern coast of Sicily until they made contact with the advancing Americans. It was an audacious plan. That night, the four men negotiated their way onto the beach, slithering across the sand until they reached one of the beached boats. Working silently and swiftly, they gently eased the boat down the beach and into the water. Lodge continued:

> 'And now we made our fatal mistake. Unforgivable for men trained in boat work, explainable only by the state of our nerves. Instead of swimming the boat out quietly for several hundred yards we suddenly all tried to jump and scramble into the boat and to grab the oars. We made such a clattering noise this time that the guards were awakened and the alarm was given.'

Sharman recounted what happened next in his report:

> 'A machine gun opened up but it was being fired at random. I estimate that there were some eight to ten men firing at us and the boat was hit repeatedly, so much that it became waterlogged and it was obviously sinking, so we dropped into the sea using the boat for cover. We discussed the situation, and decided that we had no choice but to surrender. We attempted to do this, but the firing did not diminish and I was hit in the armpit so the captain swam ashore and managed to persuade the Italians that he had surrendered. I crawled back into the boat as my right arm was useless and Mason swam ashore towing the nearly sunken boat almost to the beach, whereupon I stood up to jump into the sea and step ashore. Whilst in this position I was hit again in my thigh. I fell into the sea and the Italians dragged me ashore. We were all taken back to Gioia Tauro where my wounds were dressed and my three companions were then taken away, presumably they left for the north the next morning.'

Lodge, Bridgeman-Evans and Mason were transported by train to a prison camp at Capua, north of Naples, but they made another bid for freedom later in the year, and this time they were successful.

In his review of Operation *Chestnut*, Bill Stirling acknowledged that it 'was only partially successful'. He continued: 'Few of the tasks were carried out and the value of damage and disorganization inflicted on the enemy was not proportionate to the number of men, amount of equipment, and planes used.'

Nonetheless, given the short notice with which the operation had been planned, and the fact that late changes were made to *Chestnut*, Stirling was not downhearted. 'It provided valuable experience for future operations and pointed out the pitfalls which are inevitable in any operation which is the first of its kind,' he wrote.

Chapter Six

On 14 July 1943, the 2SAS parties deployed on Operation *Chestnut* received a radio message informing them: 'Augusta taken by British troops. They are now making good progress northwards along the East Coast.'

The previous day, as the SRS had partied in Augusta's public garden, the town was secured by 17 Brigade of the 5th Division. On their left flank, the 50th Division had advanced towards Lentini, 15 miles north-west of Augusta, but encountered stiff resistance from the Italian Napoli Division.

On that same day, 13 July, it was decided by XIII Corps to send in the SRS to Catania, in a role similar to that at Augusta, an advance assault force to gain a bridgehead in the town.

'Maps were issued and full briefing for the operation was carried out,' remembered Lieutenant Peter Davis of the SRS:

> 'Since the job was intended to be done that same night [*sic*], we were kept busy preparing our equipment and weapons. While all the time we wondered to ourselves what the outcome of it all would be. Catania was a town larger than any which had hitherto been captured, and moreover, was still some twenty miles ahead of our forward troops. The risks attached to this coming operation seemed greater than those which we had had to face previously, and even before we knew the full facts of the situation, grave doubts milled through our minds to the effect that an unusually tough proposition lay ahead of us, from which we would indeed be fortunate if we were allowed to return safely.'

The briefing given to the officers of the SRS instructed them to land at Cape Mulini, 8 miles north of Catania, where with other elements of the Special

Paddy Mayne took his men on a training run up Mount Etna (seen here from Catania in 2023) in August 1943 but no one could keep pace with their C.O.

Service Brigade they would form a bridgehead on the coast for the landing of 17 Brigade north of Catania.

The operation was planned for the night of 14/15 July, but at 2000 hours the SRS learned that the landing had been cancelled. The relief, noted Davis, was 'considerable'. He heard later that XIII Corps had made the decision after intelligence reached them that German forces were deployed in strength in Catania (the town did not fall to the Allies until 5 August).

For the rest of July, the SRS were in camp, 2 miles north of Augusta. Other than the odd air raid, the war diarist recorded 'Nothing to Note' for most days. They underwent light training, and then on 6 August they gathered for a briefing on Operation *Walrus*.

The objective was Cape Ali, approximately 25 miles south of Messina in the north-east corner of Sicily. The SRS's instructions were to land in two LCIs (Landing Craft, Infantry) and destroy the road over the railway at Cape

Johnny Wiseman, MC, in the centre, front-row, poses with his men in 1943, not long before most were killed by a shell at Termoli.

Ali, blocking road and rail communications for as long as possible. The LCIs would land 100 yards south of the target, and it was anticipated that the assault would last no more than ninety minutes. Number 3 Troop would lead the attack, supported by 2 Troop and Captain Muirhead's mortar section.

However, the operation was cancelled a few hours after the briefing. 'We were aboard the LCIs and ready to sail,' remembered Captain Derrick Harrison. 'Five minutes later, news came that the Eighth Army was moving so fast up the coast that it was feared we might cut them off instead of the Germans. It was "job off" again.'

Instead, a frustrated SRS entrained for Cannizarro, just north of Catania, and Paddy Mayne established his HQ in what had been up until recently the opulent home of a wealthy doctor and prominent fascist. The men made themselves comfortable in the courtyard and adjoining lemon grove. It was

Taken from the height to the north of Bagnara, this photo in the 1930s gives an idea of the vines in which the Germans concealed themselves as the SRS advanced up the winding road.

an idyllic spot, and also, remembered Sergeant Bill Deakins, an educational one: 'Amongst the possessions of the previous doctor owner were a number of coloured illustrations of many kinds and types of venereal diseases, with the consequential after effects. Enough to put one off sex for the rest of one's life.'

Not that the SRS had many opportunities for courting local women in their new billet, but they did have access to alcohol, and their commander led by example. 'We had many episodes with Paddy [Mayne] in Catania,' said Signaller David Danger. 'One night we had a party and we were all bedded down in the courtyard of this house. We didn't have tents. Suddenly Paddy started pelting us with flowerpots and we had to take evasive action.'

Mayne gave life his all, whether it was partying, training or fighting. A few days after he had been boisterously showering his men with flower pots, he raced them to the top of Mount Etna on a training exercise. 'Average time to climb Etna from end of road, 2¾ hours,' recorded the SAS war diary. 'Major Mayne, DSO, 2 hours.'

Alex Skinner won a Military Medal at Cape Murro di Porco but was killed at Termoli.

On 20 August, the war diarist recorded that Mayne had been awarded a bar to the Distinguished Service Order he'd received in North Africa. It was a reward for the accomplishment of the two operations in Sicily, the citation praising his 'courage, determination and superb leadership which proved the key to success'.

There was a clutch of other decorations, including the Military Cross for Lieutenant John Wiseman for his dash on the gun battery at Capo Murro di Porco, and six Military Medals. Privates Alex Skinner and John Noble were among the recipients, as was Sergeant Andy Frame, who was still recovering from his shoulder wound sustained in Augusta.

Three days before the medal announcements, General Harold Alexander, the Allied Deputy Commander-in-Chief, cabled Winston Churchill to inform him that 'the last German soldier was flung out of Sicily'. 'Flung' was not wholly accurate. The Germans had affected a disciplined withdrawal, overseen by their commander, General Hans-Valentin Hube. In the first sixteen days of August, the Germans had transported almost 40,000 personnel from Sicily across the Straits of Messina to the Italian mainland, along with 9,000 vehicles and 12,000 tons of stores.

While the Germans were evacuating Sicily, the Allies were considering their next move. General Dwight Eisenhower, supreme commander of AFHQ, discussed the invasion of Italy with British and American chiefs of staff, and decided the following: General Montgomery's Eighth Army would land on the toe of the Italian boot, just across the Straits of Messina from Sicily, while Lieutenant General Mark Clark's Fifth US Army, whose initial orders were to land between Taranto and Bari, were now to assault the Bay of Salerno, on the west coast of Italy, 30 miles south of Naples. The two armies would comprise 15th Army Group under the command of General Harold Alexander

Early on the afternoon of 1 September, the Special Raiding Squadron broke camp, marching to Catania docks and embarking in two LCIs, each of which could transport a maximum of around 200 men. One of the craft developed propeller trouble a few miles north of Catania and the SRS were obliged to spend the night sleeping on the beach at Riposto. It took a further twenty-four hours to repair the propeller, but then there was more trouble with the second LCI, so it was decided that the SRS would be transported to their target in one LCI and four LCAs.

The target was Bagnara on the instep of the Italian boot, a coastal town at the foot of a steep terraced hillside on which were scores of vines. The main Eighth Army landings were occurring at Reggio, 11 miles south, and the job of the SRS was to secure Bagnara and the road that led from the town up to the plateau far above.

The assault force set out for Bagnara at 2000 hours on 3 September, two-and-a-half hours behind schedule because of the transport difficulties. Everyone was more tense than usual. Peter Davis recalled:

> 'The dull blue glow of the operational lighting gave a sinister and grotesque twist to our faces as we grouped around to complete our final preparations. Around 2am we began to feel restless, knowing full well that we were near the area in which our landing and attack were to take place. The troops were assembled each in their respective holds, fully equipped, and merely waiting for the word to disembark.'

Captain Harrison recalled waking at around 0200 hours and, peering over the starboard beam, discerning the Italian coast and then the shape of hills. Harrison and Davis, and the rest of 2 Troop, were in the second wave. The honour of leading the assault fell to 3 Troop and two sections

Sid Payne, seen here on the right in 1945, was a member of Two Troop.

of 1 Troop, whose orders were to land on the most southerly stretch of Bagnara's mile-long beach, then secure it and the main road that ran along the beachfront.

Sergeant Joe Schofield described what happened as the first wave closed on the target at 0400 hours:

> 'We approached the beach quietly under darkness in an orderly fashion but our [LCA] skipper was one of those people who always carry a red tail light no matter what vehicle he is travelling in. His Number One, I should think was ex-Guards by the sound of his voice, which carried to a terrific pitch when angry orders were hastily issued to the crew. However, if the enemy heard us, or rather heard the noise of a craft, they thought it was an aircraft and they put up a steady flak barrage.'

Bagnara itself was silent. Some thought it ominously quiet, and asked themselves if the beach was mined. 'No one knew if the beach was mined or not,' said Signaller Alf Dignum. 'Paddy Mayne was first up the beach, walking all the way, and by the time we'd followed him up there was only one set of footprints. And it was bloody hard for me, being so short, keeping up with his footsteps!'

Private Alex Griffiths agreed: 'When we hit the beach the first man off was Paddy Mayne. We were all thinking about mines but he walked right up the beach with the rest of us all trying to get behind him. He might not have been a particularly nice fellow, but as a soldier he was the greatest.'

Mayne soon realized they had been landed in the wrong place, on the northern beach instead of the southern one, though it later emerged that this was an unintended stroke of good fortune as the southern beach had been heavily mined by the Germans.

Once the assault party had secured the road, and found the town to be devoid of enemy forces, they signalled to 2 Troop on the LCI lying offshore. Harrison instructed his section to move into position as the vessel approached the beach, and when the ramps lowered they were quickly down and onto dry land, moving up towards the promenade like 'scalded cats'. They crouched in the doorways of the restaurants and cafes that lined the seafront, a popular destination for working-class holidaymakers in the summer season. A signaller from HQ Section found Harrison and told him his presence was requested by Major Poat, who had landed with the second wave.

Poat had already given Lieutenant Davis his instructions as they crouched behind the stone wall that separated the beach from the promenade. Poat told him:

> 'Look here. Paddy has decided to alter the whole plan because we have been landed so late and so far out of position. We have no time to clear the town properly now, and we certainly don't want to find ourselves caught in it in daylight, so we will push straight through, and hold the bridge which crosses a deep wadi bed at the foot of the main road running up the mountain to the north of the town. One Troop has already moved off to cover the northern approaches of the town, while Three Troop will be doing the same to the South. Now get cracking and for heaven's sake, don't delay!'

An aerial reconnaissance of Bagnara in 1943. The SRS landed on the left hand end of the beach and headed swiftly inland up the steep and narrow streets.

The improvisation impressed Davis, who attributed it to Mayne being a 'born leader' and a 'real genius', with 'the ability to make split-second decisions, which later events prove to have been as equally wise as those normally hammered out over a period of days'.

He gathered his section and explained their orders were to head north, up through the town, and secure the road bridge. Captain Tony Marsh, commanding 2 Troop, was already leading his section towards the bridge, and Harrison's section would bring up the rear.

One section of 3 Troop, meanwhile, headed south to search for the enemy. Lance Corporal Albert Youngman remembered approaching with caution a railway tunnel cut into the hillside just beyond the southern extremity of the beach: 'Dawn was just breaking [and] we didn't know what to expect. We had been warned of a German presence in Bagnara but so far we had seen none. Were they hiding in the tunnel? But we didn't find any. They were just chock-a-block with locals.' Members of 3 Troop reassured the frightened townspeople that they were safe and that their town would soon be clear of Germans.

As dawn broke over Bagnara, Peter Davis led his section up towards the bridge where Tony Marsh and his men had set up defensive positions. As they climbed the sharply rising streets, the shutters of a house were thrown back and an old man yelled excitedly: '*Inglesi! Inglesi! Buono, molto buono!*' Otherwise, the streets were deserted and there was no sign of any Germans. 'All seemed quiet, and the peace of that lovely autumn morning slowly began to reassure us,' said Davis. 'Perhaps, after all, the place was unoccupied by the enemy.'

Suddenly, Davis heard a question from his runner, Private Johnny Hair. 'Is that 3 Troop on the road behind us?' he asked his officer. Probably, replied Davis, who then turned to make sure. The soldiers were ascending the street below in single file, about 300 yards from Davis's section. The light was still imperfect as Davis scrutinized the soldiers through his binoculars; there was no mistaking their headgear: they were Germans.

Between Davis and the Germans was Harrison's section, and they were also aware of the men to their rear. Sid Payne was the last man but one in Harrison's section. He recounted:

> 'The chappie behind me tapped me on the shoulder and pointed to his ear, then down the road. I could hear marching. So I tapped the bloke in front of me and signalled to him, and we all spread out on the road and round this bend came the first ranks of this column of Germans, carrying their rifles at ease.'

The Germans were engineers, recently arrived with orders to blow Bagnara's bridge to hinder the British invasion force at Reggio. They had no idea the enemy had beaten them to their objective. 'They got quite a surprise,' remembered Payne. 'They weren't even looking in our direction and we began laying it down. It was like being at the funfair when we opened fire.'

The Pont di Caravilla bridge in Bagnara, one of the first objectives of the SRS, which they captured before it could be blown by the Germans.

The few Germans who weren't killed in the initial fusillade fled back into the town and gladly surrendered to Lieutenant Pat Riley and his section of 1 Troop.

The firing had echoed through the narrow streets and up into the terraced hillside overlooking Bagnara. If there were Germans in the town, they were now aware they had company.

Harrison's section re-formed and pushed on, climbing the steep staircases that linked one street to the next. They found Davis and Marsh at the bridge, their men spread out in defensive positions, and Harrison was informed that Mayne was waiting for him around the next bend. Harrison found his commander sitting on a doorstep studying some aerial photos of Bagnara. Mayne invited Harrison to join him on the step, showing him one of the photographs and explaining the likely reaction of the Germans. He said they would counter-attack down the winding road that led from the hillside to the seafront. What Mayne couldn't predict was the strength of any putative attack. He had already sent 1 Troop on ahead, and his orders to Harrison and Davis were to dig themselves in even further up the road.

As 2 Troop began to ascend the road, 1 Troop came under fire from the Germans positioned on the terraces above. A salvo of mortar bombs landed close to where Bill Fraser had established his Troop HQ, killing two of his signallers, Charlie Richards and William Howell. Further down the road, a tracer bullet clipped Harry Poat's trouser leg but killed Thomas Parris walking behind. The maps in Poat's pocket caught fire, but he continued to issue orders as he calmly patted out the flames.

Davis led his section up the winding road, a sheer rocky cliff-face to their right and on their left the terraced hillside. As they rounded a bend, Davis cursed at the sight of the straight road that stretched ahead for 300 yards. 'It was indeed an unpleasant position in which to be caught if they should open on us,' said Davis. 'Our only hope was to press on round the next bend in the hope that there the lay of the ground would be in our favour.'

They were midway along the road when a flurry of mortar bombs fell on the road, landing slap bang between Davis and his lead section and the sub-section led by Corporal Bill Mitchell 30 yards to the rear. As the smoke cleared, a German machine gun opened up. Mitchell withdrew his section back down the road, while Davis screamed at his twelve men to advance. Davis recalled:

> 'We doubled like mad things down that road in a vain search for cover from those murderous eyes on the hillside above. We rounded a slight right-hand bend as the bullets started to chip into the asphalt beside us, our pleading eyes frantically searching for some trace of cover. And there, barely fifty yards ahead, was the most wonderful sight we could wish for. It was a small one-roomed peasant cottage on the left side of the road.'

Once inside the cottage, Davis realized that they were temporarily out of harm's way, but still horribly exposed to the well-camouflaged German positions visible from the window. The enemy were dug in 200 yards ahead, at a point where the road crossed a deep gully and doubled back to the left at a sharp angle, affording them views of the town and the hillside road. Davis was sure the cottage would come under mortar attack, but no bombs fell, leading him to suppose they were either out of sight of the mortar observation post or were too close to permit accurate fire. Knowing they had

The Maria Santtissima del Rosario church in Bagnara, looking in 2023 as it did when the SRS filed past in 1943.

the men trapped in the cottage, the Germans turned their attention back to Bagnara, mortaring it at regular intervals and sending the occasional burst of machine-gun fire on to the road to keep Mitchell's section pinned down. A radio message from Davis was received; it may have been garbled, but it was misinterpreted because Mitchell led his men up the road. Davis was horrified when he saw them break cover; this wasn't what he had ordered. The Germans saw Mitchell's section at the same time as Davis. One of the men with Mitchell was Corporal Bob Lowson, who remembered that suddenly 'the earth fell in on us' as a flurry of mortar bombs rained down. The salvo was just short and only one man received a slight wound. Mitchell screamed at his section to withdraw. 'We all started to run back down the road,' said Lowson. 'And then their machine guns opened up.' Mitchell was shot in the side, and all the rest of the section except Lowson and one other soldier were also hit. 'Most of the boys could get down the road unaided,' recalled Lowson. 'We went back and dragged [Snowy] Kirk and [Paddy] Glacken to safety.'[7] Meanwhile, Davis and his men made themselves as comfortable as they could in the cottage:

> 'We sat up in the brilliant sunshine of that cloudless autumn morning and commenced eating our breakfast from the tiny ration packs we had brought with us. It is true to say that we were lulled into a sense of security by the gentle rustle of the vine leaves in the morning breeze, and by the rich, clean smell of the grapes.'

As the morning passed and the Germans sent no more fire the way of the cottage, Davis formulated an escape plan. Accompanied by Sergeant Andy Storey and Private Charlie Tobin, he would dash for a culvert 50 yards away. Once safely inside, they would crawl back down the road until they were out of sight of the German machine guns. The remaining men would follow in pairs at regular intervals.

As the three men prepared to rush from the door, Davis turned to Lance Sergeant Bill McNinch and issued some last-minute instructions. Storey and

---

7. A nerve in Kirk's leg had been severed by the bullet, and such was his injury that he didn't rejoin the SAS.

Photographed in 2022, the beach at Bagnara where the SRS landed in the early hours of October 4, not on the southern end as planned but to the north.

then Tobin stepped out of the cottage and into a burst of fire from a German machine gun. Tobin was killed instantly. Another machine gun opened up, then another, and for several minutes the men huddled against the wall in the face of the firestorm. Then the firing stopped and the enemy reverted once more to attacking the town below.

Most of the mortar shells fired by the Germans dropped harmlessly on Bagnara. The rest of 2 Troop was dug in among the vine terraces, while 3 Troop were still checking the tunnels for any Germans. Private Alex Griffiths of 3 Troop rounded up a couple of engineers from the earlier ambush and marched them to the SRS HQ. 'These Germans were starving, poor sods, asking me the whole time for food,' Griffiths said. 'I didn't have any to give them but one of our lads gave them some biscuits and that made them happy. We didn't really need to guard them, [as] they had no intention of escaping.'

Davis and his section remained in the cottage until dark. Then, cautiously, soundlessly, they crawled out one by one. Davis paused to examine Tobin's body and remove his rifle and personal belongings. Back in Bagnara, they were greeted warmly by comrades who had given them up for dead. After some food and a debrief, Davis wrapped himself in an old blanket and tried to rest. "But it was a long time before sleep eventually came,' he remembered. 'Again and again I would hear dinning through my ears that murderous burst of fire which had sent Tobin to his death.'

While Davis and his section had been trapped in the cottage, Captain Harrison and his men had spent the day positioned a few hundred metres down the road. They had edged their way up, negotiating the hairpin bends that at times left them feeling horribly exposed. They were the moments when the German snipers, concealed among the foliage in the hillside, had a good field of fire. One marksman drew a bead on Sergeant James McDiarmid, who was shot in the ankle. In spite of his wound, the Scot helped his men to pull back. He was subsequently awarded a Military Medal, the citation for which related that he 'ordered his men to carry out a right flanking movement and … covered the withdrawal of his subsection from a position which was continually under fire. He then crawled back, rejoined his men, and led them into the hills.' McDiarmid's resolve was said to have 'greatly inspired the men under his command'.

Harrison's section left the road, fighting their way through the undergrowth, where they were at least concealed from the enemy snipers. 'I decided to take up a defensive position among the trees covering the town below us,' he recalled. Harrison sighted two Bren guns looking north towards the small village of Pellegrina, the direction from which Paddy Mayne anticipated any counter-attack would come. It was now mid-morning and the sun was hot. Sid Payne remembered that they dozed under the shade of some vines, their slumber shattered now and again by the German battery not too far above them. They were evidently unaware of the British soldiers a few metres below, and were directing their fire onto Bagnara. 'There were a lot of grapevines and we stayed in there,' recalled Sid. 'But above us there was a plateau with a German battery up there and we could hear them chatting to each other.'

At some point in the day, a platoon of Germans was seen coming down the road from the direction of Pellegrina. Harrison ordered his two Bren gunners to open fire; the Germans scattered back up the road and didn't reappear for the rest of the day.

Charlie Tobin, far left, and Bob Lowson, foreground, playing cards in the desert in 1942. Tobin was killed at Bagnara and Lowson just avoided serious injury.

Now, however, the German battery above Harrison's section was aware of their presence. Unable to bring their guns to bear on the British, one of the Germans threw a grenade that exploded close to Harrison's position. He scanned the hillside with his binoculars and caught sight of what looked at first glance like 'a grey boulder'. He kept his glasses trained on the shape and after a few moments it moved. 'It was a rather fat German in field grey crawling cautiously along and hands and knees,' said Harrison. 'He was followed at intervals by a number of others.' Harrison counted ten in total, all of them making slow progress towards a grassy bank.

He decided to withdraw his men back down the hillside to a more secure position. There they spent the night, unmolested by Germans but also unaware of the fate of Davis's section.

Down below and to the south of the town, 3 Troop had what Sergeant Joe Schofield remembered as a 'comparatively quiet day'. Having secured the railway station and searched the tunnels and found only frightened civilians, 3 Troop took up defensive positions in case of any German thrust from the south.

In fact it was the British who were closing in on Bagnara, but the advance element of 15 Brigade, the 1st Yorks and Lancs Regiment, was held up by a destroyed bridge a few miles south. Between them and Bagnara was a German rearguard detachment, positioned at the southern end of the tunnel in which the townspeople of Bagnara had sought shelter. Evidently they were unaware that the SRS enemy had launched an amphibious night-time assault on the town; they were expecting any attack to come along the road from the south.

The night of 4/5 September passed without serious incident. At first light, Harrison and five men headed back up the road to try to locate the battery below which they had spent much of the previous day. One of the men who accompanied Harrison was Sid Payne. 'It was a tough climb, forcing our way through the bushes and what not,' he said. 'At one moment we rested, and as we looked out across Bagnara a British cruiser hove to right in front of us. The gun swung round and let fly at the battery above us. The shells came whistling over our heads. They made a horrible sound.'

Harrison had a signaller with him and reported his progress to Major Poat, but when he tried again a couple of hundred yards further up the hillside there was no signal. They pressed on, wriggling through the undergrowth on their stomachs, Harrison and his men keyed up and expecting to spot the battery any moment. All they encountered was a road and then a handful of excited Italians, some of whom could speak English, having worked in the USA for many years. Jumping for joy, they told the SRS that the Germans had withdrawn less than an hour ago. Harrison and his men sat on the verge facing the sea, relief coursing through their bodies. Suddenly, a file of soldiers appeared from round a bend. 'My instinct was to drop to the ground and open fire, but for some reason or other I did not,' said Harrison. 'Neither did they. Warily we approached each other, alert for the first false move.'

The soldiers weren't Germans, but Britons, members of the Green Howards Regiment. 'Where the bloody hell have you lot been?' asked Private Bob McDougall, one of Harrison's men. 'We have been sitting here waiting for you.' A major strode up to McDougall and upbraided him for his language. Then he broke into a broad grin. It was the son of McDougall's boss back in Liverpool.

The 1st Yorks and Lancs Regiment appeared in Bagnara in the early afternoon of 5 September, having fought off the Germans and made their way through the railway tunnel. It was raining by now, and the men of the SRS were anxious to leave a town that had cost them five dead and more than twenty wounded.

Peter Davis sought out one of the men in Bill Mitchell's sub-section, Bob Lowson, and together they walked up the hillside to bury Charlie Tobin. 'Charlie was my best pal,' recalled Lowson. 'We'd been in the Middle East Commando together and joined the SAS at the same time. [He was] a great Irishman who loved his cards.' Lowson and Davis buried Tobin behind the cottage on the road in which he had lost his life. 'When I got back down the lads were all asleep on the railway station,' recalled Lowson. 'In the corner was an Italian local with a little squeezebox playing "Amapola".[8] I could have bloody cried.'

There was little time for reflection or sentimentality. The SRS were roused from their sleep, and Davis said that at 1700 hours on 5 September they marched out of Bagnara to the south under a grey drizzle. They boarded two LCIs bound for Messina in the north-east of Sicily and the men stood on deck watching the hills receding, thinking of what they endured in the previous thirty-six hours.

Paddy Mayne wrote a report of the operation, which had been codenamed *Baytown*, in which he stated:

> 'Most of our opponents were Germans and only a few Italians were seen. Some belonged to a Grenadier regiment [29th Panzer Grenadier Division], some to a Jaeger battalion and many were Sappers, left behind to blow up roads and bridges.
>
> 'In general, German troops were of good physique and experienced. Some had fought in Africa and some in Russia. One prisoner belonging to the Jaeger battalion stated that his unit was equipped with British vehicles.
>
> 'Prisoners questioned told us that they were completely unaware of our landing, and were taken by surprise. It can therefore be presumed that had our landing taken place at 0200 hours, as intended, the whole position would have been cleared with much less casualties.
>
> **'Fighting Conditions**
> 'Fighting consisted mainly of long range sniping and long range G [gun] fire.

---

8. 'Amapola' (meaning 'poppy') was a romantic song that had been popular since the 1920s, being much-recorded, including versions by the Jimmy Dorsey Orchestra and Deanna Durbin.

'Fifty of our casualties [inflicted on the enemy] were from very accurate mortar shelling; 30 from G fire and 20 from sniping.

'On the whole our shooting was good and many spectacular results were obtained. The country was broken and hilly with very good cover.

'Miscellaneous

'The inner communication worked very badly. The reasons given are one) bad batteries two) weakness of 38 sets in hilly country three) HQ squadron had no 48 set, one being left on the LCI.

'It is considered, however, that better training and more resourcefulness on the part of the signallers would prevent a reoccurrence of such poor results.'

Lieutenant Davis concluded that the Bagnara operation had been a success:

'As had been envisaged, by our landing behind the main defences of the enemy, and forcing him to retire to his prepared positions in the hills, our occupation of the town had greatly facilitated the advance up the coast of our main forces, who, in the course of a single day had been able to press forward against only slight opposition to the extent of 12 miles.'

Chapter Seven

Three days after Paddy Mayne and his Special Raiding Squadron sailed away from Bagnara, Italy officially surrendered. A few hours later, the first Allied troops landed on the beaches just east of Salerno, while in the southern city of Taranto, British and American troops also came ashore, including the bulk of Lieutenant Colonel Bill Stirling's 2SAS.

However, a small party of 2SAS had earlier been withdrawn from the regiment's North African camp at Philippeville and 'isolated'. There were thirteen men in total, including Lance Corporal Harry Challenor. 'We were getting frustrated at no action; excited at every wild rumour that an operation was coming and then despondency when it "blew over",' said Challenor, known as 'Tanky' because in the Commandos he had worn a Tank Corps beret after losing his own. 'Then the atmosphere changed.'

Aside from Captain Philip Pinckney there were three other officers: Captain Pat Dudgeon and Lieutenants Tony Greville-Bell and Thomas Wedderburn, whose father, Ernest – a prominent Edinburgh lawyer – had been knighted in the 1942 New Year's Honours. Wedderburn was an asthmatic, a condition that had not prevented him indulging his enthusiasm for mountaineering while reading law at university. The officers had some say in selecting the men for a forthcoming operation to be launched on 7 September: Pinckney chose Private Len Curtis, 'a John Bull Londoner' and football enthusiast, Sergeant Bill Foster, who had impressed him during Operation *Chestnut* in Sicily six weeks earlier, and his trusted pair of sergeants, Horace Stokes and Tim Robinson. The latter duo had known Pinckney since their days in No12 Commando in 1941, and Robinson regarded his officer as 'a man of great courage, intelligence and kindness'.

Stokes was aware that Pinckney was carrying a back injury, sustained when he had parachuted into Sicily in July. Pinckney was surreptitiously taking

Harold Challenor (left in 1945), nicknamed 'Tanky', took part in Operation Speedwell and was one of the few who avoided execution.

medication for the injury – 'a freezing mixture' – which Stokes begged and borrowed from a medical unit in Philippeville, but it was evident to Stokes that Pinckney was in no fit state to make another jump. '[Bill] Stirling knew nothing of the injury and if he had known he would not have let PHP [Pinckney] jump,' said Stokes.

In his stick, Greville-Bell selected Sergeant George Daniels, who had been with him on the Lampedusa raid, and a Scottish soldier of Italian extraction, Corporal Pete Tomasso, whose family owned one of Glasgow's most popular ice-cream parlours. The other men assigned to what was codenamed Operation

Corporal James Shortall, left and circled, was one of the men of Operation Speedwell who was caught and executed.

Speedwell were Corporal James Shortall, Harry Challenor and Private Bernie Brunt. The latter was the youngest member of the thirteen, a 21-year-old Yorkshireman, who had participated in Operation *Chestnut* in July, an eighteen-day adventure that had made the British newspapers.

According to Challenor, the thirteen men spent a few days at the start of September undergoing punishing route marches on the hills overlooking the 2SAS camp. 'Trekking, map reading and explosive drill and making up charges figured heavily,' he said. Then, on 5 September, Bill Stirling addressed the men and 'gave us the first inkling of what it was all about'. Most of the briefing was given by Captain Eric Barkworth, the 2SAS intelligence officer.

They would be dropped by parachute to blow up trains, preferably in tunnels, and disrupt communications in the mountainous area of northern Italy bordered by Genoa, La Spezia, Bologna and Florence. The objective was to impede the flow of armoured reserves reinforcing German resistance to the Allied invasion and the US Fifth Army landing at Salerno.

'Any questions?' asked Barkworth when he had finished. Greville-Bell had one: 'What about getting back?' Barkworth grinned: 'That's up to you.'

Sergeant Daniels, nicknamed 'Bebe' in honour of the famous Hollywood actress, appreciated such directness. Having volunteered for the SAS in early 1942 from the Northamptonshire Regiment, he felt comfortable in his new unit. He reflected:

'I found it suited me better. You had to use your own initiative. There was a sense of excitement. I never fancied getting killed for some obscure reason. With the SAS you knew exactly what your target was. You did your own intelligence work. You knew the odds. It was all yours, and that's what I liked about it.'

The men arrived at Kairouan airfield on the morning of 7 September and split into their respective parties. Bill Stirling attached himself to Stick 1, led by Pinckney, and to keep their minds from wandering he suggested they play cards. They used Greville-Bell's parachute as a card table and the game they played was baccarat. 'I lost a £100 to Bill Stirling in the three hours before we took off,' said Greville-Bell. 'But we couldn't spend our money then anyway.'

Captain Dudgeon was in charge of Stick 2. He took his five men into an olive grove and opened a bottle of whisky. For more than hour, said Challenor, 'there was a great deal of aimless chatter about the respective merits of the Italian wine and women'.

At 1800 hours, they began to make their final preparations. Greville-Bell fitted his parachute to his back and Pinckney checked his small-arms equipment. He was wearing US Army overalls, to which he had strapped a combat knife.

Horace Stokes (back far-right) and next to him Tim Robinson pose with other commandos circa 1941. Both went on Operation Speedwell.

He carried his favourite .30 calibre carbine and a .45 Colt automatic pistol. 'I don't feel too good about this one,' Pinckney confided to Greville-Bell. 'But then, I always get that feeling at the start, you know, the feeling that every operation might be the last.'

The thirteen men boarded two Albemarles, the first of which took off at 1830 hours. Pinckney and the six men in his aircraft settled down for the five-and-a-half hour flight north to the remote DZ halfway between Florence to the south and Bologna to the north. In his report on the operation, Greville-Bell described the approach to the DZ: 'No flak was encountered as far as I was aware. The pilot took very evasive action crossing the coast. Pilot did one run up over DZ, turned in and stick left on SE course. Height believed to be 7,000 feet. Visibility bad, heavy ground mist and gusty wind, 20–25 mph.'

Greville-Bell was the penultimate man in the jumping order. First out was Pinckney, followed by Stokes, Robinson, Curtis, Tomasso, Greville-Bell and Daniels. Each man knew the drill on landing: first of all, hide their parachutes, jump jackets and helmets. The number one to jump, in this case Pinckney, would roll back to number two, who would not move until located, and these two would then roll back to number three, and so on, until the stick was complete.

Pinckney leapt into the darkness the moment the red jump light turned green, hurling himself out with a bellow. Then Stokes went, and as he descended he saw a lake as the mist parted beneath him. The stiff breeze began to push Stokes out of line as he approached the ground. He heard Pinckney's voice: 'Watch your drift, Stokes, watch your drift.'

Stokes acknowledged his officer's advice, but there was little he could do to change his path: 'The bloody wind blew me straight into the side of a chimney and when I hit it I knew I'd really done myself some damage, which felt like a rupture.'

It was a most unfortunate landing for Stokes, who had picked out an isolated farmhouse, the only building in the area. 'I needed to get out as quickly as possible but I was really tangled so I had to drop out of my harness.' As soon as he crashed to the ground, cursing and rubbing his sore knee, Stokes hobbled away from the farmhouse, convinced his exertions must have been heard for miles around. Was it his imagination, or was that the faint wail of an air raid siren he heard over the wind?

Stokes hadn't followed the procedure about rolling up the stick, but luckily he encountered Sergeant Tim Robinson within minutes. Robinson had just avoided a tree, landing flat on his face as he took evasive action. Apart from a few cuts and bruises, he had landed unscathed.

So had Corporal Pete Tommaso, who had jumped after Robinson. Tommaso later wrote in his report of the operation:

> 'I landed about 75 yards from an isolated farm on the side of a hill. Captain Pinckney landed about 300 yards from me round the side of the hill, but out of sight. He called me by name, which was unusual, as there were two NCOs (Sergeants Stokes and Robinson) between us, and I answered. I waited for an hour on them coming up. All this time I could hear noises coming from the direction of the containers. After about another 10 minutes had passed, Sergeant Robinson found me waiting where I had landed. I asked him about Captain Pinckney and Sergeant Stokes, but he said he never saw them. Both of us then decided to make for the place where the noise was coming from, after waiting another 20

> minutes. On arriving there, we found Lieutenant Bell, Sergeant
> Stokes, Sergeant Daniels, and Pct [parachutist] Curtis getting the
> containers emptied.'

Greville-Bell was in considerable pain, having been buffeted by the wind on his descent towards the lake. 'I put into action the drill for falling into water,' he remembered. 'I got out of my harness and was hanging by my hands, and then a gust of wind brought me back to the hills again. So when I actually landed I was clinging on by my hands to the harness and my chute caught in the top of a tree.'

He was swung violently round by the sudden brake on his descent, breaking two of his ribs as he collided with the tree. His head also smashed against the trunk, but his helmet absorbed most of the impact, leaving him dazed.

Pinckney wasn't the only absentee. They were also missing a pannier. Sergeant Daniels remembered:

> 'An air raid warning sounded when we came down. We stayed in
> the area for two hours looking for Captain Pinckney, and the last
> container, which was very light and probably had drifted a long
> way. Then we moved off into a large hill, and after hiding the
> containers, stayed undercover for the next day. Lieutenant Bell
> was still in great pain.'

Pinckney's fate puzzled them, particularly as he had called out to Tomasso after landing, but they held out hope he would be found when dawn broke.

A hindrance to Operation *Speedwell* was their lack of radio communications. They had been inserted so far north that they were out of range of 2SAS HQ in North Africa, and when dawn arrived on 8 September they were ignorant of the impending announcement of Italy's capitulation. After weeks of secret negotiations, the Italian armistice with the Allies was promulgated by General Eisenhower on Algiers radio at 1730 hours local time on 8 September. 'All Italians who now act to help eject the German aggressor from Italian soil will have the assistance and support of the United Nations,' declared the commander-in-chief of Allied forces in the Mediterranean.

At first light on 8 September, the six SAS men were concealed in some woods halfway up a hillside south of the village of Castiglione. Greville-Bell had slept well for a couple hours, his slumber deepened by half a grain of

Bernard Brunt (pictured) and Pat Dudgeon were executed by the Germans after hijacking a German car and killing the occupants.

morphine he had taken at 0400 hoursm. His ribs soon started to hurt, however, so he took some more morphine.

He was more troubled by the disappearance of Pinckney. He concluded that the captain must have been disorientated on landing, perhaps by the gusting wind, and had set off on the wrong bearing and was now lost somewhere in the mountains. No trace of him was found when some of the men searched the DZ at dawn. A couple of hours later, the SAS men watched from the hillside as a truck arrived and a squad of Italian soldiers combed the area around the lake. 'I now decided to split the party into two, instead of three, since I was not certain that I should be able to continue owing to

Taranto harbour, pictured in 2022, was where 2SAS disembarked in Italy on September 10 1943.

injuries,' wrote Greville-Bell in his report. He, Daniels and Tomasso would comprise one party, and Robinson, Stokes and Curtis the other. They spent a couple of hours dividing up their equipment, which consisted of 16lb of plastic explosive, 4½lb of cheese, two tins of sardines and some tea and biscuits per party.

For a few hours, the men remained undercover in the woods, then in the late afternoon they marched together up the hillside. Shortly before dusk, they separated. Greville-Bell and his party headed west in the direction of Poretta, while Robinson led his stick south-east towards the Bologna–Prato railway line.

Greville-Bell was still in great pain, dosed up on morphine, so he handed over command temporarily to Sergeant Daniels. 'I had a good landing, I never had any trouble landing,' recalled Daniels. 'To be honest I always thought I was built for the SAS because I had a rough upbringing and was fit before I joined the army. I used to walk miles and miles. With Pinckney disappeared and Tony injured we had to organize and I was in charge.'

Studying the map, Daniels and Greville-Bell picked as their first target a tunnel on the railway line south of Poretta.

Greville-Bell recorded the events of the next forty-eight hours in a journal:

> 'Crossed mountain and lay up just south west of second lake.
>
> 'Walked again, but was in great pain, and was finished after two miles. Decided to have one more night's rest and if not able to keep up would send Daniels and Tommaso on without me. One grain morphine in two doses.
>
> 'Ribs better and beginning to knit so decided to carry on, though every time I fell there was an unpleasant grating noise. Typical days [*sic*] food at this time [was] biscuits, 1½oz cheese per man, lots of water. Country very broken and precipitous in this area and going very slow, much cover however. Reached mountain above Road junction south of Poretta going past several houses as dawn was breaking.
>
> 'Head now normal, took over again from Daniels. Large German armoured column came through road junction and took road east. Moved south parallel with road and railway and went on to railway to recce point for demolition.'

The three men observed the tunnel for a day from their vantage point on the hillside. It was unguarded. Evidently, they were so deep inside enemy territory that the Germans saw no reason to post sentries at the tunnel's entrance. Daniels considered himself something of a demolitions expert, having learned the art at Philippeville under the tuition of Captain Pinckney. Daniels explained:

> 'His baby was blowing railway lines. We knew how much explosive we needed to cut a rail. A gun cotton block would cut the rail but a pound of plastic high explosive [HE] was a better cutting charge. Plastic HE hadn't been out long but it was so good because you could mould it to a line. You just moulded it to the line and of course join it up with cortex.'

Once the three SAS men had crept into the tunnel, they went to work with swift efficiency, laying four charges on the line, each of 1lb of plastic HE.

Tony Greville-Bell and George Daniels, seen here in 1944, overcame many setbacks to turn Speedwell into a success.

'The clip-on detonators were based on the similar idea to [a] fog signal,' said Daniels. 'If there was fog the train would set off a small charge, which obviously wouldn't harm the line or train. We adapted this idea only ours did harm the train!'

Having laid the charges 150 yards inside the tunnel, the three men walked briskly out and climbed the hill to their vantage point. 'At 2205 hours we heard a fairly fast train approaching from the north,' wrote Greville-Bell in his report. 'It entered the tunnel and set off the charge, causing the power lines to short circuit. We were unable to see the results, but judging by the noise, I believe the train to have crashed.'

The men remained on the hillside for the rest of the day and to their satisfaction no trains came along the line, while from inside the tunnel they heard sounds of industry as soldiers and civilians strove to clear the wreckage.

They left the area at nightfall, heading south-east until they reached a stretch of track on the Prato–Bologna line, 2 miles south of the village of Vernio. They moulded 6lb of plastic explosive to the rail there and attached a pull switch. The three then withdrew and waited. 'This was unfortunately a complete failure,' recalled Tomasso. 'We were told that southbound trains were on the right hand line … and pulled the switch as the train approached, but it was on the left hand line.'

That failure, and their growing hunger, dampened the men's spirits. They were revived, however, on the morning of 19 September when they passed through vines on which grew grapes and tomatoes.

That evening they laid another charge with a fog signal, and this time it was a success. Greville-Bell counted twelve carriages careering off the line, taking with them a large section of the track. As they withdrew up the mountainside, they heard the screams and groans of the injured.

The next day there was what Greville-Bell described as a 'terrific concentration of rail traffic in this area waiting to get through on [the] single line'. Satisfied with their handiwork, the three soldiers headed south.

Towards evening on 23 September, they reached the village of Vaglia, only to discover a German motorised column was parked on either side of the only road. 'We had to go down this road to get out of the other side,' said Daniels. 'We walked down the column and we could see them in camp beds, but we were so far behind the lines that they didn't even challenge us – even with rucksacks on – because they thought we were natives.'

Autumn had now arrived in northern Italy, and with it came a drop in temperatures and the start of some heavy rainfall. They crossed the River Arno on 28 September in a stolen boat, and the next day encountered an Italian who had recently escaped from a concentration camp, where he had been imprisoned for his anti-fascism. He fed the SAS men and put them in contact with a group of partisans, among whom was a doctor, who examined Greville-Bell's ribs and confirmed that two were fractured. 'Still can't breathe properly,' he wrote in his journal.

The partisans loaned Greville-Bell some civilian clothes, and on 4 October he walked into Florence. Some of the city was out of bounds to civilians, mostly the districts north of the Arno that cuts Florence in two. Greville-Bell found a cafe on the Piazzale Michelangelo, the celebrated observation point on the south side of the river. He ordered an ice cream, then a beer, which, as he noted in his operational report, was 'very bad'. The tables either side of him were occupied by German soldiers. Most were drunk, only paying for about

Tim Robinson was best friends with Stokes and it was a wrench to have to leave him in Italy.

one beer in five. That wasn't all that Greville-Bell observed. There was a rumour that the city's bridges had been prepared for demolition, and that was evidently true.

The next day, the SAS men laid the last of their charges on the line between Florence and Incisa, and according to a subsequent partisan report a train was blown off the tracks.

With their explosives gone, the three men began the long trek south to the Allied lines. It took them a month, and it was a brutal, punishing experience. Daniels suffered from dysentery, Greville-Bell's ribs caused him pain, and cold and hunger were constant companions. Eventually, on 13 November, after seventy-two days behind enemy lines, they crossed the River Sangro and staggered into the forward positions of a British artillery unit. 'They asked where we had been and we said we'd been quite a few miles away from here,' recalled Daniels. He was awarded a Military Medal for his contribution to the success of Operation *Speedwell*, the citation noting that because of his leadership when Greville-Bell was incapacitated, he 'made the operation a great success when failure seemed likely'.

Having parted company from their comrades on the evening of 8 September, Sergeants Tim Robinson and Horace Stokes and Private Len Curtis agreed, recalled Robinson, that the 'best plan would be to travel at night until we reached the objective and for four or five days after, and then continue in daylight'.

The objective was a railway line near the village of Vernio, which they reached on 15 September 15. Robinson recounted:

> 'We moved to the entrance and before attempting to lay the charges we put our ears to the rails to see if we could detect any trains that might be coming in a short while. We got no vibrations so while Stokey got busy fixing the charges, Curtis covered him to the south and I to the north.'

Having set the charges, the three SAS men retired to a spot on the high ground above the tunnel. Within minutes, Robinson said, they heard the sound of a train:

> 'We waited with bated breath. Then a lightning flash, followed by one almighty bang that reverberated around the hills. Complete silence, then a few odd noises for a couple of minutes. Suddenly a rattle of rifle fire broke out in the area that we had just vacated. Who was firing at who, I did not know. They were certainly not shooting at us.'

Robinson, Stokes and Curtis had no more explosives, so their focus switched to exfiltration. Moving east, Robinson said that on 21 September they 'literally bumped into two Italian soldiers, who to our amazement, were overjoyed to see us after learning that we were British, the reason being that since Italy had capitulated we were not enemies of theirs anymore'.

For the next fortnight they relied on the generosity and kindness of Italian peasants, who fed and sheltered them, but Stokes became increasingly lame on account of the knee he had injured upon landing. He knew he was holding up Robinson and Curtis, and on 6 October told his companions he was going no further. Robinson conceded it was the right decision; they left Stokes in the care of a farmer, who spoke English, having lived in the States. 'Said our farewells and left at 0900 hours,' recalled Robinson. 'I did not like leaving him but he understood … there was a strong feeling of regret among the three of us at having to split as we had become a team who trusted one another implicitly and there was a true blend of friendship right from the start of our being together.'

Robinson and Curtis marched south for the rest of October, at times in the company of Allied POWs who had been released from their Italian prison camps after the armistice and were also seeking to reach friendly lines.

On the last day of the month they heard the sound of artillery fire, a welcome indication that they were near the front line, even if it meant they would have to negotiate their way through the German positions. 'Cautiously carried on through the woods with the German 88 shells going one way overhead and the British 25 pounders the other,' said Robinson. 'Eventually emerged from the woods close to some old sheds, behind which was the outskirts of a village.'

There was a sentry on duty, and he was wearing khaki. They had made it, reaching the village of Frosolone after a trek of some 300 miles. The Canadians there, astounded at the adventure they heard of, lavished food and cigarettes on Robinson and Curtis.[9]

The other section of Operation *Speedwell*, commanded by Captain Pat Dudgeon, had come to earth without physical injury. 'I had landed in a small wooded copse on a scrub-filled mountainside,' remembered 'Tanky' Challenor. 'I began to walk on my line bearing to link up with Mr Wedderburn, using a low whistling sound as a prearranged means of identification. Within an hour we had all linked up.'

That was the good news; the bad news was that it was soon apparent to Dudgeon that they had dropped many miles from the intended DZ. Instead of landing a miles south-west of Borgo Val di Taro, they were near the village of Barbarasco, approximately 30 miles south.

---

9. Sergeant Stokes recovered from his knee injury and continued his journey, but he was caught in Rome in March 1944. He escaped from a POW camp in Germany but was recaptured before being liberated in April 1945. After the war he was a greengrocer and pub landlord, and died aged 65 in 1986. He kept his wartime exploits secret until revealing the facts recorded in an old journal on his deathbed; this journal being adapted and published by his son in 2013 as *No Ordinary Life* and becoming a best-seller.

The six soldiers concealed themselves in the copse and slept for the rest of the night. At dawn on 8 September, they collected the containers and laid up for the rest of the day. At dusk, they dispersed in pairs: Challenor and Lieutenant Thomas 'Tojo' Wedderburn went in the direction of the La Spezia–Bologna line; Sergeant Bill Foster and Corporal James Shortall made for the Genoa–La Spezia line;, and Dudgeon and Bernie Brunt set off for another section of the Genoa–La Spezia line. 'A rendezvous was arranged for seven nights ahead, at a point on a stream between Pontremili and Villafranca,' recalled Challenor.

Challenor and Wedderburn spent two days and nights trekking across the Apennine mountains. They were wearing the same American boots and overalls as the men of Stick 1 of *Speedwell*, eating the same food and carrying the same amount of plastic explosive. What distinguished them were their small arms; Greville-Bell and his men preferred the carbine, but Challenor had over his shoulder a German MP40 machine pistol (Schmeisser).

The pair's march ended when they came to a railway tunnel long enough to lay charges at a good distance between the 'up' and 'down' lines. Wedderburn and Challenor kept the mouth of the tunnel under observation for several hours until they were satisfied it was unguarded, descending from their vantage point at midnight.

'It was pitch black inside' as they entered the tunnel, remembered Challenor:

> 'We laid our first charge on the outside line of the down-line to La Spezia. We then walked for a considerable distance and planted another charge on the up-line. We were making our way back to the entrance when we heard a train coming. It was travelling on the down-line where we had placed the first set of charges. Running and falling we just cleared the tunnel mouth as the train thundered in. With a rumbling BOOM! the explosion echoed down the tunnel. There followed a crashing, smashing, banging, screeching sound of metal piling up. As we left the scene we both heard it – a train on the up-line! We listened in awe. BOOM! Again, more crashing noises and then an eerie, awful silence. We had claimed two trains and undoubtedly blocked the La Spezia to Bologna line as ordered. A very long hard climb into the mountains followed

until Mr Wedderburn called a halt and we rolled into our sleeping bags deep in the undergrowth.'

Wedderburn and Challenor reached the rendezvous site on 15 September. Dudgeon's instructions were that no party should wait more than three days at the map reference in the event that one or more teams failed to arrive. By 18 September, there was no sign of Dudgeon and Brunt, or Foster and Shortall, so Challenor and Wedderburn reluctantly departed. They had with them the last of their plastic explosive, which they used on a stretch of line between La Spezia and Pontremoli. 'The explosion echoed round the hills,' remembered Challenor. 'We laughed like hell and headed South. Now that the Italians had surrendered we could walk by day as long as we kept to the Apennines away from German troop movements.'

The intention of Sergeant Foster and Corporal Shortall was to sabotage the line between La Spezia and Genoa. It was an attractive line, one that hugged the Italian coast and allowed passengers stunning views of the sea. To reach it from the DZ was hazardous for the two SAS men, involving fording the River Vara and crossing a main road that ran north to south. This road was heavy with German traffic heading south towards the main fighting around Salerno, and villages were teeming with military personnel.

On 20 September, Foster and Shortall approached the village of La Foce, just north-west of La Spezia. Temporarily billeted in the village was the146th Regiment of the German 65th Infantry Division, and they regarded with suspicion the two men who walked boldly down the road. Unlike the Germans who had taken no notice of Tony Greville-Bell and his team when they walked past, this regiment was more alert. Foster and Shortall were ordered to halt, and a search was made of their rucksacks. Inside, according to post-war testimony of the German officers involved in Dudgeon's arrest and execution (and used during war crimes trials), they discovered 'two pistols with ammunition, two different types of explosive charges, detonators, various types of fuses, and tools'.

The two British soldiers were driven to the 65th Infantry Division's HQ at Ponzano Magra, 10 miles north-east of La Spezia, which was situated in a villa next to the Vaccari ceramics factory in the centre of the town. Neither co-operated during their interrogation. Foster and Shortall were handed into the custody of the local Carabineri under the command of 47-year-old Maresciallo

Vito Romaniello. On the evening of 20 September, Romaniello recalled, a 'German officer ordered me to put the two English soldiers in in the cell saying they were saboteurs'.

At around midnight, the Germans returned and removed one of the two prisoners for interrogation. An hour later, they returned the SAS soldier and took the other, also for questioning. This went on throughout the night.

Foster and Shortall were interrogated over several days, but the Germans found them unresponsive to their questions. It is likely that messages were being sent during this time, asking for instructions on what to do with the pair. They were not escaped POWs; they were commandos, evidently engaged on a sabotage mission, and since 18 October 1942 the punishment for such men was death. On that date, Hitler had issued his Commando Order (*Kommandobefehl*), a reprisal for a report that German prisoners had been killed on the Channel Island of Sark by British commandos, among whom were Pat Dudgeon and Geoffrey Appleyard. According to the commandos, their prisoners were not killed in cold blood but as they tried to escape to warn their comrades. It is more likely that Hitler issued his Commando Order because he was becoming troubled by the number of their raids on the French coast and wished to eliminate this threat as much as he could.

Only a few copies of his order were distributed, but word soon spread among German forces that captured commandos should be 'ruthlessly destroyed'. The Commando Order continued:

'This is to be carried out whether they be soldiers in uniform, or saboteurs, with or without arms; and whether fighting or seeking to escape; and it is equally immaterial whether they come into action from ships and aircraft, or whether they land by parachute. Even if these individuals on discovery make obvious their intention of giving themselves up as prisoners, no pardon is on any account to be given.'

Foster and Shortall's fate was probably decided by Lieutenant General Gustav von Ziehlberg, commander of the 65th Infantry Division.[10] The officer with

---

10. Gustav von Ziehlberg was subsequently convicted of involvement in the Stauffenberg bomb plot to assassinate Hitler in July 1944, and was executed by firing squad.

the task of executing the pair was a Captain Sommer. Late in the morning of 30 September, Sommer ordered Lance Sergeant Fritz Bost to assemble a firing squad to shoot two British soldiers who 'had landed by parachute in civilian clothes'.

Bost organized the detail and, as instructed, marched them into the grounds of the ceramics factory next-door to the villa that housed the HQ of the 65th Division. Sergeant Bill Foster and Corporal James Shortall emerged dressed in 'airmen's overalls'. They were led up a slope at the back of the factory. Bost observed the pair. The sergeant was tall and athletically built and his comrade was slim with an angular face and prominent dark eyebrows.

No doubt the two SAS NCOs had already understood their fate, but it was confirmed by Sergeant Gerhard Tochtermann of the German Military Police, who stood before them and declared that as 'members of a sabotage party [they] were to be shot by order of the Fuhrer'.

One of the two prisoners said something, but Sergeant Bost spoke no English and anyway he wasn't interested. Bill Foster was grabbed and pushed towards a lone tree, to which he was tied. One of the Germans attempted to slip a blindfold around his eyes, but the sergeant turned his head and refused to cooperate. He continued talking. Captain Sommer asked the interpreter, Lieutenant Emil Grether, what the prisoner wanted. 'A priest,' said Grether. 'We have no time for that,' sneered Sommer.

The firing squad trained their rifles on Foster, but just before the order to shoot was given he flinched. Sommer ordered him to be blindfolded, and Foster was then shot. He was still alive from the salvo, so Sommer applied a coup de grace. Shortall was then led towards the tree as Foster's body was dragged to one side. The cord that had pinioned him was now used to bind Shortall. The corporal said nothing in the final few seconds of his life.

A few days after the execution of Foster and Shortall, Sergeant Fritz Bost was told by Captain Sommer that 'the execution squad would probably have to function once again' because two more British saboteurs had been apprehended.

The pair had been detained at a routine German checkpoint at the summit of the Cisa Pass, about 30 miles north of La Spezia. The driver of the vehicle was a broad-shouldered man who responded to the guard's question by explaining in fluent German that he was on his way 'to fetch my paybook and work ticket from my unit'. The guard took them at first glance for Italians, many of whom came through the pass each day. But then he looked again at the driver's beret, of a type he had seen on no Italian. According to post-war testimony of the German officers involved, it was coloured and on the front 'was a badge with two wings'. Furthermore, the short blond-haired man in the passenger seat did not have the complexion of a local soldier. The guard ordered the pair out of the car.

Pat Dudgeon and Bernie Brunt had hijacked the vehicle a short while earlier, killing the two German soldiers inside and hoping it would take them well clear of the railway line they had earlier sabotaged.

Traces of the blood of the Germans was on Dudgeon's tunic, and inside his rucksack was 40lb of explosive. He and Brunt were interrogated at dawn the next morning, but the German officers later testified that the questioning was 'broken off since it had led to no result'. The Germans had learned from Foster and Shortall that whoever these men were, they were not the talkative kind. A message then arrived to the effect that the bodies of two German signallers had been found in a ditch not far from the Cisa Pass. Dudgeon and Brunt declined to comment, but the Germans drew their own conclusion. Lieutenant General Ziehlberg ordered the execution of the pair.

It was decided to shoot them on the spot rather than waste time transporting them to the ceramics factory. Dudgeon and Brunt must have heard from the guardhouse the hammering as two thick posts were sunk into the ground, and in the meantime the officer in charge of the firing squad, Lieutenant Preissner, selected his detail, choosing 'old, experienced soldiers'. Dudgeon was shot first, having been allowed a moment to kneel and pray before his execution. Then it was Brunt's turn. He declined an invitation to pray.

Thomas Wedderburn and Harry Challenor had reached the outskirts of the city of L'Aquila by the start of December, around 250 miles south of where they had dropped three months earlier. Lance Corporal Challenor had suffered for some of that time from malaria, a disease he picked up at 2SAS's mosquito-infested base at Philippeville. Despite his entreaties to leave him, Challenor was still in the company of Lieutenant Wedderburn, who had found them shelter at a farm owned by Mama Domenica Eliseo, 'a Mother Earth figure' in Challenor's estimation. She and her two grown-up children were already harbouring three escaped British POWs.

Shortly before Christmas, there was a noticeable increase in German activity in the area as their forces retreated north in the face of the advancing Allies. Wedderburn decided it would be prudent if the fugitives split up, so he was taken in by a woman called Philemena and Challenor moved to a cave close to Domenica Eliseo's farm. On 27 December, the Germans raided Philemena's house, killing her and capturing Wedderburn. Challenor fell into German hands a few days later as he trekked south by himself. He later recalled that he was roughed up and 'then hauled into a car and driven to a large building in Popoli where I was marched to a courtyard and shown a wall pock-marked with bullet holes and obvious blood stains on the ground … the officer told me that I was not a solider but a spy and I would be shot'.

Challenor may have been saved by his malaria, which returned with a vengeance, and he was moved to a POW hospital. For several days he was very sick, and in all probability the Germans who had threatened him forgot all about him. Nonetheless, Challenor decided it would be wise to escape as soon as he felt strong enough, which he did, dressed as a woman. He was helped by his fellow hospital inmates, who regarded his plan as mad but admirable. Challenor recounted:

> 'One of the lads had a pair of knee length black woollen socks which he had obtained while on the run during the early days. Another chap produced a large square of material which he kept all his belongings in. It made a perfect shawl. We then gathered all the needles and thread we could find and spent hours sewing up one of the lice-ridden blankets from a bed. When I put it on it made a passable skirt, coming just below my knees.'

Challenor had worked out his escape route, which entailed passing through the back of the cookhouse where the rations were delivered. It was the way used by the local women who worked at the hospital. But would he be able to walk out of the front gate of the hospital without being detected for what he was?

'I need not have worried. I passed through the gate without the sentries giving me a second glance.'

Challenor remained on the run for three months, until in April 1944 he met British troops advancing north through Italy. 'It was the greatest moment of my life,' he said. Someone produced a mug of hot tea, and another handed over a tin of cigarettes. 'All I could say over and over again was "I've done it, you bastards".'

After seven months, Operation *Speedwell* was finally over.

Chapter Eight

The thirteen men who had deployed on Operation *Speedwell* on the evening of 7 September 1943 left behind the rest of 2SAS in North Africa. They soon followed to Italy, not by parachute but rather by troopship.

Five squadrons under the command of Major Felix Symes were transported across the Mediterranean to Taranto aboard an American cruiser, one vessel among a large convoy steaming towards the port in the 'heel' of Italy. 'We were not long out of Africa when we heard over the ship's intercom that the Italians had packed in,' remembered Charlie Hackney.

The squadrons disembarked at Taranto on 10 September with orders to operate as a reconnaissance force for the 1st Airborne Division.

Under Major Oswald Cary-Elwes, A Squadron drove north-west in their jeeps in the direction of Mottola. The SAS had been using jeeps since the summer of 1942, procuring a fleet in Cairo. They were American Willys Bantams, admired for their good suspension, brakes and fuel economy. Rugged, mobile and light, they were equipped by the SAS with Vickers K machine guns taken from obsolete Gloster Gladiator biplanes. Capable of firing 1,200 rounds per minute, the Vickers were mounted fore and aft in the jeeps.

The men of 2SAS were still familiarizing themselves with the jeeps, having only acquired them a few weeks earlier, but their guns were soon called into action. On 11 September, A Squadron ran into Germans just outside Mottola, and the next day they overpowered a detachment of Russian troops serving in the Wehrmacht.

On 16 September, Cary-Elwes rendezvoused with Captain Roy Farran's D Squadron and handed over A Squadron to his command. Cary-Elwes had orders to return to North Africa to deputise for Bill Stirling, who had been summoned to London for high-level discussions about the possible of expansion of the SAS into a brigade.

Roy Farran was a born guerilla soldier who led his 2SAS squadron with bold panache from Italy to France.

In Taranto, 2SAS were under the command of Brigadier John Hackett, Commanding Officer of 4 Parachute Brigade. Hackett, who had been David Stirling's boss a year earlier in North Africa, had a respect for the versatility and valour of the SAS. His orders to Major Felix Symes were that B Squadron should 'take up a position on the Bari road and hold up a reported German column'. The enemy never showed, so B Squadron's commander, Captain Peter Power, a 32-year-old Irishman who had been a tea-planter in Ceylon before the war, embarked on a series of reconnaissance patrols on behalf of the 1st Canadian Division. It was an unsatisfactory task for 2SAS, one that didn't make best use of their talents. If Bill Stirling had had his way, his regiment would all have parachuted into northern Italy to attack the enemy's lines of communications. This was what they had been trained for, not to undertake reconnaissance patrols.

Power led B Squadron to Bari, on the Adriatic coast, on 21 September to await further orders, although it was hoped that they might establish a base in the port, from which to launch amphibious raids. That ambition never materialized. The frustration felt by B Squadron was also being experienced by C Squadron, commanded by Captain John Gunston. They didn't even have any jeeps, so were reduced to patrolling in a 1916 Renault truck with a

Sandy Wilson, front centre, poses with his troop shortly before Termoli, a battle in which Wilson lost his life.

maximum speed of just 10mph. On 20 September, Gunston and his men were shipped back to North Africa.

Roy Farran's orders from Brigadier Hackett were for D Squadron to advance north along the Massafra road that led towards Bari. It was an eventful few days, which Captain Farran described in his operational report:

'11th Sept: Patrolled up coast road to Ginosa crossroads, two minutes before head of German transport column arrived. Successfully ambushed them, capturing two trucks and 42 men, and destroying 10 vehicles and 6 men.

'12th Sept: Squadron moved to east of Castellaneta position at 1100 hours. One patrol under Lieutenant Mackie operated in area south of Castellaneta with a foot patrol from B Squadron.

'14th Sept: Amalgamated with remains of A squadron, had wireless fitted, and phantom apparatus attached. Moved late in afternoon towards Gionosa. Hunted German M/C [motorcycle] combinations without success, and reported Ginosa crossroads clear.

'16th Sept: Lieutenant Jackson left at first light for area Ginosa and obtained good observation on road. Bumped German patrol near Ginosa, scattered them with fire from Vickers gun.

'17th Sept: In the afternoon, Lieutenant Mackie went with foot patrol through tunnel to penetrate German positions on the other side of the hill … the jeeps which transported them as far as the tunnel were fired on by MGs. Patrol bypassed German sentries and got behind German positions.

'18th Sept: Lieutenant Jackson's troop crossed SAS bridge and bumped A/tk gun position. Shot them up and then got a good position on a flank to observe Matera … Lieutenant Huggett and SSM [Squadron Sergeant Major] Mitchell penetrated German positions at Grottole, shot up a patrol in the village and captured a prisoner.'

Mitchell was recommended for a Military Medal by Farran, the request being signed off by General Montgomery in November 1943. 'In these engagements, SSM Mitchell's dash and courage were outstanding and his example stimulated all of those under his command to the highest degree,' stated the citation.

On 22 September, D Squadron reached Bari and billeted with B Squadron in a school. Their instructions were to await the arrival of 4 Armoured Brigade, under whose command they were to henceforth operate. Two days later, Farran was off again, and invariably he soon ran into some Germans. 'Got jeeps in fire position and pasted German positions for 30 minutes at 150 yards range,' he wrote in his report.

On 25 September, a day described as 'gruelling' by Farran, D Squadron embarked on a reconnaissance west of the main Foggia road and came under heavy mortar and machine-gun fire. 'The Sqn scattered helter-skelter but eventually reassembled and withdrew,' recorded Farran. By the end of the month, Farran and his men were laagered 12 miles south of Bari, where they 'rested and refitted'.

October began with torrential rain, and on the second day of the month Farran received orders to lead his squadron north to Termoli, an eastern

A German lorry burns on a bridge over the river Biferno during the fighting for Termoli in October.

Italian coastal town 125 north of Bari. Two miles south-east of Termoli, the River Biferno empties into the sea, and General Montgomery was determined that the Germans would not use this geographical feature to build a solid defensive position. If the Allies captured Termoli, they would be able to outflank their enemy and force the Germans to withdraw further north.

As Farran and his squadron drove north towards Termoli, Major Paddy Mayne's Special Raiding Squadron was also headed to the port under Operation *Devon*. They were part of an amphibious assault by the Special Service Brigade, which also included 3 Commando and 40 Royal Marine Commando.

The brigade had sailed from Manfredonia further down the coast on 2 October, the 207 officers and men of the SRS transported in LCI 179. The first to land on the long sandy beach to the west of Termoli was 3 Commando. Signalman Bryan Woolnough recalled that it was a dry and unopposed landing:

'We set down at 2:30 AM and it was obvious that the Germans were asleep and completely unaware of the imminent raid. Usually to protect a coastal beach, mines would have been laid and this was not the case. Having established a perimeter bridgehead without any firing the way was clear for 40 [RM Commando] and the SRS to land.'

Woolnough signalled in the SRS at 0245 hours, but the LCI ran aground on a sandbank 50 metres from shore and it wasn't until 0300 hours that Mayne and his men came ashore, issuing the password 'Jack Hobbs', to which the commandos replied 'Surrey and England'. The Germans were not only oblivious to the famous cricketer, but were also in the dark as to what was unfolding to the north of them. Termoli was garrisoned by elements of the 1st Parachute Division, dug in on four strong positions along the lateral road facing south-east. They hadn't entertained the possibility the British would make an amphibious attack to the west of the town.

Lieutenant John Tonkin of 3 Troop led his B Section south-east towards the Biferno. His orders were to capture the bridge and hold it until relieved by the British 78th Division. Meanwhile, 1 Troop, under the command of Captain Bill Fraser, was heading down a road south to Campomarino. The instructions issued to 2 Troop were to push 4 miles inland south-west of the town and attack the Germans as they withdrew. The commandos' orders were to seize and hold the centre of town. Colonel John Durnford-Slater, commanding 3 Commando, and Brian Franks, brigade major of the Special Service Brigade, approached the railway station, less than a quarter of a mile inland. 'We heard an engine making starting noises and, hurrying, found it facing in our direction,' said Durnford-Slater. Franks leapt up into the cab of the train and ordered the driver to raise his hands. Durnford-Slater recorded:

'His train never did make its scheduled trip northward. The coaches behind the engine were loaded with German troops, fast asleep. We woke them up and made prisoners of them. They took a lot of rousing and could scarcely believe what was happening. They thought they were thirty safe miles behind the front lines.'

The strip of beach at Termoli, photographed in 2023, was where the commandos and the SRS landed in the early hours of October 3.

The German paratroopers belonged to Battle Group Rau, led by a major of that name, whose total strength was in the region of 400 men. Rau was captured in his pyjamas; he hadn't even had time to destroy important papers. His troops dug in on the road to the south-east began to pull back, just as Tonkin and his men appeared out of the darkness. 'When we landed at Termoli we sort of turned left and we had to go and hold these two bridges to enable the British army coming up,' recalled Private Alex Griffiths, a member of Tonkin's section. 'The Germans started retreating but of course they were coming past us in their hundreds.'

There was confusion on both sides; shouts of 'Jack Hobbs', which went unanswered, and then bursts of firing. Tonkin's section reached the main road down which the Germans were streaming at 0500 hours. A vehicle appeared heading north and the British opened fire. It was a staff car, now containing one dead officer and another wounded. Three other Germans had their hands raised.

Tonkin's section continued and, according to the operation report, at 0530 hours they 'engaged troops in five trucks. 2 in[ch] mortar sets fire to one truck but is knocked out.'

The Germans then went from being the hunted to the hunter, aware in the first strands of dawn that they had the numerical advantage. 'When daylight came I saw lots of Germans and I remember thinking "Cor, look at all those prisoners those blokes have got!",' Private Griffiths recounted. 'Then all of a sudden they opened fire and we were taken prisoner. They disarmed us and we wandered along with them feeling pretty fed up.'

Most of Tonkin's B Section was captured,[11] although six men managed to hide among scrub in a dried river bed, emerging only when they saw their comrades from A Section arrive. This force of 3 Troop then chased the Germans down the road, killing one and taking nine prisoners. One sub-section was led by Sergeant Ernest Goldsmith, known as 'Buttercup Joe' on account of his habit of singing the words to the popular folk song. He was an ebullient soul, though a terrible card player, and had proved his mettle on many occasions since joining the SAS eighteen months earlier. Captain Bob Melot, a 48-year-old Belgian who had joined the regiment at the same time as Goldsmith – having impressed David Stirling with his intelligence-gathering behind enemy lines in Libya – was shot in the shoulder. He was with HQ Squadron, advancing with 3 Troop to gather intelligence for Paddy Mayne. Seeing Melot fall, Goldsmith dashed forward 'with great daring and initiative' and carried him to safety despite the attention of German riflemen. Goldsmith was subsequently awarded a MM for his conduct, the citation praising 'his very high standard of leadership and his courage' throughout the events at Termoli.

The members of 1 Troop, meanwhile, were advancing down the Termoli to Campomarino road. Rounding a bend, they were confronted by a German half-track with a short-barrelled 10.5cm gun. The enemy vehicle was destroyed, but the SRS then came under fire from a farmhouse. The order went out to bring up the mortar section under Captain Alex Muirhead. Section leader Sergeant Reg Seekings later stated:

> 'He [Muirhead] was good, I had a lot of confidence in our mortar team. I wanted some fire brought on a building from where I was. I

---

11. Alex Griffiths spent the rest of the war as a POW, but Lieutenant Tonkin escaped from captivity a few days later.

stood up but I was still under cover of this hedge and embankment from the Germans. Over the wireless I said to Alex, "Can you see me?" And he said, "I see you". So I said, "Aim on me, plus a short 25 [yards]." He put the first shell straight through the bloody roof. I said another one and he did the same and he rained a few bombs down on them.'

This was at 0600 hours, and for the next hour the Germans held out before withdrawing from the mortared farmhouse to a building further down the road. They were chased by mortar and small-arms fire. Seekings continued:

'Then the Germans decided to come out and that's when we first knew what they were. [They were paratroopers, veterans of the capture of Crete in 1941, under the command of a physically imposing major.] When the major saw us he pointed at another officer being carried on a stretcher. It was his young brother. He said to me "Please shoot him, there's nothing we can do to help him". And [Sergeant] Chalky White took his revolver and shot this Jerry through the head. It was the right thing to do because he was dying.'

In total, 1 Troop had killed ten Germans and taken another twenty-one prisoner.

By 0900 hours, the fighting was all but over and Termoli was now controlled by the Special Service Brigade. Two hours later, 3 Troop advanced down the Campomarino road and made contact with the advance elements of 11 Infantry Brigade, soldiers who, had the amphibious assault not been such a success, would have walked straight into the sights of the German 1st Parachute Division.

The men of 2 Troop had encountered no enemy soldiers as they advanced south-east from the landing beach. The greatest obstacle in their path, remembered Lieutenant Peter Davis, was the terrain: 'The rain had spread a slippery coating over the ground on which our smooth rubber soles obtained no grip whatsoever.' Davis and his men had to scramble up and over a railway embankment that ran parallel to the beach and promenade on which they had come ashore. Away to the left of Davis's section were those of Captains Tony Marsh and Derrick Harrison. The latter's instructions were to head 3 or 4 miles

The remains of the truck hit by a shell in the Via Regina Margherita di Savoia in Termoli.

south to high wooded ground. Having negotiated the railway embankment, Harrison helped up Captain Muirhead and his mortar section (soon after, they received orders to head east to the farmhouse where 1 Troop was engaged). Now the going became even tougher as they crossed ploughed fields that the rain had transformed into thick, cloying mud. They saw no sign of the enemy, the only sound they heard, other than their heavy breathing, being the bark of a dog from a farmhouse. They pressed on until the sky began to lighten with the approach of dawn. 'Ahead of us I could see our objective, a tree crested hill rising into the misty dawn,' said Harrison. A few minutes later, he and his men had entered a gentle valley running straight into the heart of the hill.

They came to a farmhouse, where Harrison decided to establish his HQ. Over the radio, as a jubilant Italian woman cooked ham and eggs, Harrison's signaller passed on the news of John Tonkin's capture and the wound suffered by Bob Melot. Hearing a shout from outside, Harrison investigated and saw that two of his men had caught a German. He was wearing a white armband inscribed with the word 'Kreta' in gold. The paratrooper was the first of nine to be rounded up that morning, one of whom was an officer. 'He was quite at a loss to understand what was happening,' recalled Harrison, who offered him some of his ham and eggs.

The parents of Alex Skinners, MM, one of the men killed at Termoli, visited his grave at Sangro River cemetery not long after the war.

By 1300 hours on 3 October, the battle for Termoli was over, or so it was thought. The advance elements of the 78th Division now occupied the town, and apart from desultory small-fire arms from the last German stragglers withdrawing south–west, all was quiet. The Special Service Brigade had erected a formidable perimeter around Termoli: on the right flank was 40 Commando, on the left the SRS, and No3 Commando were dug in in the centre. A total of 100 Germans had been killed in the capture of Termoli and another 150 taken prisoner. That evening, 36 Infantry Brigade began disembarking at the port; it seemed that the role of the SRS was finished. With Termoli in Allied hands, the road that led from the port to Campobasso, approximately 40 miles south, would expedite the Fifth Army's progress to Naples on the west coast of Italy.

At 1700 hours on 3 October, Mayne ordered his men back into town, into billets in a monastery opposite a public garden and 100 metres from the beach on which they had come ashore fourteen hours earlier. The officers' mess was a spacious private house opposite the monastery.

The only section absent from the snug delights of the monastery that evening was that of Peter Davis, which had lost radio contact and was still dug in 3 miles to the south-west of the town. They made themselves as comfortable as they could in a barn that had an adequate supply of straw to fend off the worst of the cold. Davis posted two sentries but 'did not take very seriously the possibility that the enemy might be up to no good on that

Johnny Wiseman, far right, in the Desert in December 1942, had a miraculous escape at Termoli.

night'. It was assumed that the Germans had pulled back, having given up Termoli.

The night was peaceful, and dawn on 4 October gave way to a watery autumnal sun. Standing outside the barn looking north-east towards Termoli, Davis saw the coastal road thick with British army transport. He was joined by one of the men from his section, who remarked: 'Well, that's about the easiest operation we've ever had.'

Later, Davis wandered over to the positions occupied by the Commandos and finally learned that the rest of the SRS had withdrawn to billets in town the previous afternoon.

Davis and his section breakfasted at the barn, after which he issued orders for them to move out. Just as they were about to depart, a shell whined over their heads and exploded 75 yards away. It left the men more puzzled than frightened. Where had it come from? 'We certainly could not explain away that shell as being one of our own,' said Davis. 'It must have been fired blind at the coast road, at a long range.'

This cemetery, photographed in 2023, was the scene of heavy fighting during the battle for Termoli.

As Davis's section strode across a meadow towards Termoli, another shell landed away to their left, and then 'something which sounded unpleasantly like a mortar bomb tore a hole in the ground behind us'.

Davis's section ran out of the meadow into a copse, taking cover behind trees as two more shells landed behind them. There were no more shells. 'We almost wondered whether we had been dreaming,' said Davis. They carried on into Termoli, passing a long line of British army vehicles, but a question nagged away at Davis: if the Germans had given up Termoli, then why was their artillery still in the vicinity?

It was late morning by the time Davis and his men were reunited with the rest of the SRS in the monastery. At midday, the Special Service Brigade issued a situation report, stating that they had been in possession of Termoli for thirty hours and during that time 'the enemy had launched no violent counter-attack, such was the success of our surprise attack'.

Not long after the brigade's situation report, a schooner and four caiques (local wooden fishing boats) sailed into Termoli harbour containing Major Felix Symes, Captain Simon Baillie and B Squadron, 2SAS. They were greeted by Roy Farran and D Squadron, who had arrived in their jeeps the previous afternoon.

German dead lie on their half-track vehicle after being ambushed by the SRS at Termoli on October 3.

Farran had been accompanied by Lieutenant Colonel Tony Simonds, commander of A Force, a cover name for a small and secretive unit of MI9 whose primary task was to assist Allied POWs to escape from Axis countries. A few miles south of Termoli, Simonds had instructed Farran to motor ahead 'to make the necessary administrative arrangements (accommodation, food, water, etc)'. When Simonds reached the outskirts of Termoli, he spotted Farran 'standing on the flat roof of a house with his arms around two pretty girls'. Simonds shouted up to Farran if he had made the necessary arrangements. 'Yes, colonel,' replied Farran. 'These [girls] are the administrative arrangements.'

The battle for Termoli had been over when Farran presented himself to Paddy Mayne during the afternoon of 3 October. The Irishman invited Farran and his squadron to share the SRS billet in the monastery, where he waited for the arrival of B Squadron, anticipating a joint operation with A Force to round up escaped Allied POWs from central Italy. There was now an unease pervading the new occupants of Termoli. As a precaution, the Special Service

John Tonkin, right, was captured at Termoli but escaped soon afterwards by leaping from a truck.

Brigade placed No3 Commando and the SRS on half an hour's notice and 40 Royal Marine Commando on two hours' notice.

Paddy Mayne asked Davis if he had seen anything unusual that morning. Davis mentioned the odd shell had dropped their way during their return from the barn, but he'd seen no sign of any Germans massing for a counter-attack. Mayne, after consultation with the Commandos, decided to strengthen the town's defences – manned now by 11 Infantry Brigade – with one section from 1 Troop (under the command of Captain Sandy Wilson) and Derrick Harrison's section from 2 Troop. They were ordered to take up a position along the railway line to the west of the town which ran parallel to the landing beach.

The shells that had been fired in the direction of Lieutenant Davis's section came from Battle Group Stempel of the 16th Panzer Division, which had reached Montenero, approximately 15 miles south-west of Termoli, on the night of 3/4 October after being alerted to the seizure of the town by the fleeing paratroopers.

They had then proceeded north to Marina di Montenero on the coast, and evidently while en route they had spotted Davis's section and sent over a few shells. Upon arriving at Marina di Montenero, Battle Group Stempel was ordered to 'thrust down on Termoli via Petacciato' while a simultaneous attack was launched from Guglionesi to the south by the Battle Group von Doering. The counter-attack was delayed because General Bernd von Doering's artillery had taken a wrong turning during the night advance and lost contact with his infantry. The Germans, going on the information brought back by the 1st Parachute Division, believed that Termoli had been taken by 'only some paratroopers with no heavy weapons'. This was correct, of course, but what the Germans didn't know was that subsequently the main British force, the 78th Infantry Division, had begun arriving.

Battle Group Stempel reached Petacciato without encountering any opposition. It was 1030 hours on 4 October, and Termoli was 8 miles to the east. By midday, the Germans were under fire from the British infantry on the western perimeter of the Termoli beachhead, and it wasn't until late afternoon that they reached the high ground (the objective of 2 Troop the previous day) overlooking Termoli.

To the south of the town, von Doering's battle group had made slow progress and was still 2 miles from Termoli when night fell on 4 October.

Nonetheless, the British were now aware that the Germans had not, as first thought, surrendered Termoli. At 1700 hours on 4 October, the forward elements of the 56th Reconnaissance Regiment, part of 11 Brigade, arrived back in the port and reported a strong German presence at Petacciato.

The Special Service Brigade diary noted on the morning of 5 October:

> 'Night 4/5 was quiet, but at 0645 hours the town and harbour were attacked by 12 E/A [enemy aircraft]. At 0930 hours Brigadier Arbuthnot (11th Brigade) stated that enemy were infiltrating through towards the town from the high ground, and that the situation had deteriorated considerably. He wished SS brigade to be responsible for the immediate defence of the town, and for suitable positions to be recced so that troops could take up positions at short notice if the position deteriorated further.'

Among the vessels attacked in the harbour by the German fighter bombers were the schooner and caiques containing the officers and men of B Squadron, 2SAS. One soldier was killed, 33-year-old Arthur Dench, who had joined the regiment from the Grenadier Guards and was batman to Captain Simon Baillie. The survivors came ashore on 5 October as the resumed battle for Termoli intensified. The British defensive perimeter was shrinking as they pulled back under heavy mortar and artillery fire from the 16th Panzer Division. The British 11 Brigade, part of the 78th Division, had been making its way north towards Termoli overland since the start of October, believing that the town was in British hands. Their progress was slow because of the heavy rain and other reasons. 'The river Biferno had to be crossed and the bridges were all blown,' recalled Lieutenant Colonel Kendal Chavasse, commanding the 56th Reconnaissance Regiment. '11 Brigade got across by scrambling and wading and the Sappers made a pontoon bridge … then it started to pour with rain and all cross country approaches became almost impossible, and no tanks had been able to cross.'

According to Lieutenant Colonel Chavasse, the 78th Division was under the impression that the 16th Panzer Division was over on the west coast of Italy, so it was something of a shock when, late in the afternoon of 4 October, on the road running north-west of Termoli, 56th Reconnaissance Regiment came up against 'the forward elements of 16 Panzer and found itself in action against German Mark 4 tanks and a considerable force of enemy infantry'.

The centre of Termoli was within range of the German armour and artillery by mid-morning and shells began to explode, the first of what would be many hundreds in the hours that followed. Soon there was another menace for the SRS. 'In the monastery we would go up to the upstairs room to do your business and you came under sniper fire whenever you went,' recalled Signaller David Danger.

Not long after midday, the Special Service Brigade received a request for 40 RM Commando to take up defensive positions to the south of the town and the SRS to do likewise to the west. Major Sandy Scratchley had recently arrived to assume command of 2SAS, and his orders were to gather as many men as possible from his regiment and establish a position on the railway line, just across from the SRS on the western perimeter. Scratchley left the Special Service Brigade HQ to fetch Roy Farran from the monastery. They returned

The Via Regina Margherita di Savoia in Termoli, photographed in 2022, where in 1943 a shell wiped out John Wiseman's section.

to HQ to find a shell had landed, killing Captain Lincoln Leese, a member of the brigade staff. Brigadier John Durnford-Slater's only remaining staff officer was Major Brian Franks, who would replace Bill Stirling as CO of 2SAS in May 1944.

Franks, Scratchley and Farran ascended a street in order to better appreciate the lay of the land and decide upon the most effective defensive position for Captain Farran to site his men. Farran recalled:

'I walked along with Franks and Scratchley. There were a lot of shells landing round about, and Scratchley half ducked. Every time a shell landed, I wanted to throw myself flat on my face. Damn it, I'd had two or three years of war, and when I heard that sort of sound ... . Franks didn't budge an inch, and that worried me, so I had to try to keep my head up.'

Also on the move was the SRS, responding to the urgent call for reinforcements on the western perimeter. Paddy Mayne instructed 3 Troop, B Section from 2 Troop, commanded by Lieutenant Peter Davis, and Lieutenant Johnny Wiseman's section from 1 Troop to board the five trucks parked in a side street between the monastery and a public garden.

First out of the monastery were the men of Wiseman's section, who climbed into the nearest vehicle, the last of the five trucks. Wiseman remembered:

> 'I put my fellows on a truck and said "right, we're going up the coast". Then at that moment I saw the colonel's [Mayne's] messenger coming to speak to me so I got out of the front of the truck to speak to him, and a shell dropped on the truck. He [the messenger] disappeared, my driver was dead and everyone on the truck was either wounded or dead. I'd lost my whole troop with that one shell. I was just talking to the messenger and he disappeared on the telegraph wires above my head. Crazy.'

The 105mm shell that destroyed Wiseman's troop was one of five that landed in the side street. Reg Seekings had been fastening up the tailboard when the bomb dropped in the middle of the truck, killing eighteen of his comrades. Miraculously, the only damage he sustained was a split fingernail. David Danger recalled:

> 'I was getting in the front truck when we were shelled very heavily and it hit the rear of the column. We could hear the shells coming over. They hit the rear [truck] and came back along the line but when we heard it coming we got out and ran into the flower bed. That's when I landed in the flower bed. I remember going down to help and there was a chap standing there with his eyeballs hanging out. He said "Am I blind?" and I said "No, you'll be ok". He was blinded. The chap next to me was wounded and we picked him up and took him to the monastery. I found later in life that I had a piece of shrapnel in my behind which eventually came out.'

One or two of Davis's men were blown into the public garden by the force of the blast, alive but badly shaken. A thick, choking smoke made survivors cough and splutter. When it began to lift, Davis saw that the 'truck had virtually disappeared, merely a twisted and shattered hulk remaining. Around it and upon it lay ghastly morsels of burnt and shattered flesh.'

Wiseman reported to Mayne that he no longer had a section to command. Mayne told Wiseman and Seekings to join his HQ Squadron, and he then studied his map. The shell that annihilated eighteen of his men had not been a lucky strike; the road where the salvo landed was obscured from the German positions outside town. He reckoned there must be a spotter somewhere inside Termoli, radioing information to a gun battery. According to Lieutenant Colonel Simonds, commanding A Force, 'the SAS found two German officers (and a W/T set) in the church tower, who had been an OP [observation post], and shot them'.

To the west of Termoli, Major Harry Poat was organizing his troops along the ridge overlooking the railway line. During the afternoon, the 78th Division had brought up a Bofors gun and six anti-tank guns, but when eleven German tanks appeared on the afternoon of 5 October, the British gunners fled.

Captain Tony Marsh led his section from 2 Troop by example, displaying what his subsequent DSO citation described as a 'high standard of courage and complete disregard for personal safety … in saving a very dangerous situation'. In the face of repeated German assaults, Marsh and his men, along with the mortars of Alex Muirhead's team, stood firm.

Mayne despatched some of the men from HQ Squadron to the front line with supplies for their comrades. 'We brought up food from the monastery to the railway yard, about a quarter of a mile, more or less along an open road covered by trees,' recalled David Danger. 'We dodged up and between the trees and carried biscuits and food. The whole time there was mortar rounds coming in and sniper fire.'

The fighting continued throughout the late afternoon of 5 October, both sides sustaining many casualties but the Germans slowly tightening the net around the defenders of Termoli. At 1715 hours, Sandy Scratchley radioed HQ for reinforcements, but all that could be mustered was a party of fifteen men from the Royal West Kents. 'Houses in the town being hit by enemy small arms fire,' noted the Special Service Brigade report.

At 1800 hours, a rumour spread that the Germans were only 200 yards away from the Brigade HQ, although this was deemed to be 'probably incorrect'. Then it was reported that a detachment of Germans, along with some armoured vehicles, was advancing along the railway line. This was correct. Roy Farran had positioned his men from 2SAS on the high ground overlooking a stretch of railway line, ten either side. Charlie Hackney was behind one Bren gun, alongside his pal, Les Nock. 'It was hellish,' Hackney recalled. 'They sent two half-tracks fully loaded with explosives on the back of a train into Termoli. We were running low on ammo so we could only fire in intermittent bursts and not all at once. They got to within about 600 yards of our position before withdrawing.'

A little further to the west, 40 RM Commando, a section of 3 Troop and the 56th Reconnaissance Regiment were positioned close to the cemetery. At one point the Germans advanced through the cemetery, held by men from 3 Troop, among whom was Lance Corporal Albert Youngman. 'It's a bloody good place to be though, a cemetery, because the headstones offer great cover,' he said. The SRS and the Germans exchanged fire in the sprawling cemetery, using not just the headstones for cover but also the trees and the mausoleums.

Then the tide of battle began to turn the way of the defenders. Troops from 78th Division had been arriving continually throughout the day. The Special Service Brigade report noted that at 1900 hours, some 6-pdr anti-tank field guns 'became available … these were put into position on the right [western] flank covering the railway line and the beach'.

Just over an hour later, a LCI arrived in the harbour. It was carrying 38 (Irish) Brigade. First ashore was its commander, Brigadier Nelson Russell, who visited Special Service Brigade HQ and was informed of the situation. He agreed to have one battalion disembark as early as possible to be ready for immediate action.

Had the Germans pressed the attack into the evening, they might still have taken the town before 38 Brigade took up position. They didn't. Instead, they withdrew for the night. The SRS war diary later noted: 'It seemed as if their troops were without the morale to advance far (again for fear of being cut off) and the attack was abandoned when the threat to the town was greatest.'

The British learned later through captured documents the extent to which the fighting had depleted German resources. At 1615 hours on

5 October, the German Tenth Army chief of staff had telephoned the 16th Panzer Division for news. He asked the divisional operations officer if he thought they would 'make it', and was informed 'that they were having a hard struggle as Termoli was built on high ground which gave the enemy observation of the approach routes and enabled him to open fire at the least movement'.

To date, the fighting had cost the 16th Panzer Division 234 casualties, and the army chief of staff was told of 'the toughness of the enemy's defence, his skilful exploitation of a terrain, and German problems in moving their armour and self-propelled equipment'. What most concerned the panzer division on the evening of 5 October was the increasing enemy air activity and the offshore artillery from a growing number of their naval vessels.

At dawn on 6 October, four Sherman tanks of 38 Brigade appeared through a cold sea mist, along with the 2nd Battalion, London Irish Rifles (LIR). A squadron of Shermans from 1 Canadian Armoured Brigade also moved west from the south. The Germans came again at first light. 'We were heavily shelled and even attacked from the air by Stukas,' remembered Major Bill Westcott of the LIR. Westcott was one of several officers who attended an impromptu Orders Group meeting in the top of the warehouse, from where they could see some of the country to the west of Termoli. Also at the meeting was Captain Arthur Komrower of 3 Commando, an old acquaintance of Westcott's. By now a veteran of the battle, Komrower provided crucial intelligence to 38 Brigade in the planning of the counter-attack. The LIR launched their assault at around 1000 hours supported by Sherman tanks of C Squadron, The Three Rivers Regiment, 1 Canadian Armoured Division, but Westcott was shot and badly wounded by a German sniper concealed among the headstones in the cemetery. Nonetheless, the attack was successful and by 1300 hours the high ground to the west of Termoli was in Allied possession.

Tragically for the SRS, one of the last offensive actions of the Germans had been a salvo of mortars bombs on the position of the SRS close to the railway embankment. One shell killed Captain Sandy Wilson and his lance corporal, Robert Scherzinger. Captain Muirhead and the SRS mortar team retaliated, sending down several salvos on the German positions in and around the cemetery.

To the south of Termoli, the fighting had been even more ferocious. At 0700 hours, C Squadron of The Three Rivers Regiment, under the command of the 3rd County of London Yeomanry, advanced towards San Giacomo, an objective of 2 Troop of the SRS on the first day of the invasion. Following was the 5th Battalion, The Buffs (Royal East Kent Regiment) to consolidate any gains made. But few were. An anti-tank screen manned by the 79th Panzer Grenadier Regiment cost the British four tanks and the Canadians two, and the advance was halted. Fighting raged for much of the day, but the German losses steadily mounted and San Giacomo was taken. At 1635 hours, the 16th Panzer Division informed its XIV Panzer Corps headquarters: 'Enemy attack in brigade strength has crushed exhausted left wing of Battle Group Doering … Orders have been given to withdraw to the area north of Guglionesi.'

Private Jack Cox of No3 Commando, who had fought gallantly in their position to the south of the cemetery, remembered 6 October well. With RAF Typhoons in the sky and the arrival of 38 Brigade, it was an 'exhilarating spectacle to behold'. He continued: 'That last day was one hell of a battle with every gun, mortar, tank, aircraft, multi small arms fire, putting up overwhelming fire power until finally the 16th Panzer Division cleared off for good. The battle for Termoli and its deep water harbour having been won.'

In its operational report of the battle, the 8th Argyll and Sutherland Highlanders commented: 'We were victorious but only by a narrow margin.'

The SRS had landed with 207 men, and of that number twenty-one had been killed, twenty-four wounded and twenty-three taken prisoner: they had been depleted by almost one-third. The two commando units, No3 and 40RM, had suffered fewer losses, with eleven men killed and fifty-nine wounded. 'Termoli was a very tough battle,' said David Danger. 'We were very lucky we didn't get wiped out.'

Shortly before sundown on 6 October, Paddy Mayne and the SRS gathered in Termoli's public garden to bury their dead. Peter Davis wrote:

'Into the gathering dusk, the silent crowd of men emerged from their billets with heads bared and softened tread. The sight of that battered truck and of those crumbled, gaping walls vividly recalled those awful few minutes of the day before. The smell of death clung heavily to the surrounding masonry. The funeral was soon over. In a quiet voice the padre read the service and dismissed us.'

On 10 October, the Special Raiding Squadron was inspected by General Miles Dempsey, commander of XIII Corps, who had first visited the unit in the spring to check on its progress. Now, nearly six months later, the men of the SRS had proved themselves in battle, fighting less as special forces, as they had in North Africa, and more as commandos.

Dempsey addressed the men and began by praising the 'brilliant' way in which they had captured the guns at Capo Murro di Porco. He then commended their courage in repelling the Germans at Termoli, explaining how the enemy had been obliged to bring up the 16th Panzer Division from Naples, on the west coast, in a vain attempt to retake the port. In addition, said Dempsey, the SRS had 'eased the pressure on the American Fifth Army', which was now advancing.

Dempsey regretted that the SRS would soon be leaving Italy – and his command – saying it had been a privilege to have them in his corps:

'In all my military career – and in my time I have commanded many units – I have never yet a met a unit in which I had such confidence as I have in yours. And I mean that!

'Let me give you six reasons why I think you are as successful as you are. Six reasons which I think you will perhaps bear in mind when training newcomers to your ranks to your own high standards.

'First of all, you take your training seriously. That is one thing that has always impressed me about you.

'Secondly, you are well disciplined. Unlike some who take on the specialised and highly dangerous job, you maintain a standard of discipline and cleanliness which is good to see.

'Thirdly, you are physically fit, and I think I know you well enough to know you will always keep that up.

'Fourthly, you are completely confident in your abilities – yet not to a point of overconfidence.

'Fifthly, despite that confidence, you plan carefully.

'Last of all, you have the right spirit, which I hope you will pass on to those who may join you in the future.'

The day after Dempsey's morale-boosting visit, the Special Service Brigade was inspected by General Bernard Montgomery, commander of the Eighth Army. His pep talk was less inspiring. On 12 October, the squadron embarked on LCI 179 for Molfetta near Bari, and not long after arriving in their new billets they were reunited with John Tonkin, who had escaped from captivity. The men needed to let their hair down after Termoli, and they obviously did, for on 21 October the war diary noted: '9pm curfew imposed. Result of general rowdyism in town.'

Chapter Nine

Unlike its sister regiment, the Special Raiding Squadron, 2SAS emerged from the Battle of Termoli relatively unscathed. Three soldiers had been wounded, none seriously, but it had been a chastening experience for Captain Roy Farran, who reflected:

> 'I had been in tank battles in the desert, I'd been in SAS operations, but infantry battles weren't my bag. We had mortars bursting all around us. Every time you moved, somebody would pop off at you with a burst of submachine gun fire. It wasn't my bag at all. I was much better in ditches shooting at people who didn't know I was there.'

On 8 October, the men of 2SAS were relieved to receive an issue of new clothing. 'Everybody cleaned up and well fed,' recorded the operational report. Farran's D Squadron remained in Termoli for a few more days, parading with the rest of the Special Service Brigade for the inspection by General Montgomery on 11 October. Afterwards, noted Farran, there was a 'Squadron feast, consisting of tomato soup, roast turkey, Welsh rarebit and fruit'.

For B Squadron, 2SAS, however, there was no time for rest and recuperation. They had arrived in Termoli by sea not to defend the town but to use the port as a base from which to launch Operation *Jonquil*.

A little over a week earlier, on 26 September, Major Felix Symes had been summoned to the Allied Military Mission at Brindisi, 70 miles south of Bari. He was greeted by Lieutenant Colonel Tony Simonds, the head of A Force, who explained to Symes that he had been instructed to rescue the thousands of Allied POWs wandering around the Italian countryside after being released on the declaration of the armistice. How many were at liberty was unknown, but it was estimated to be in the many thousands.

Simonds had divided the operational zone of Operation *Jonquil* into four areas:

A: Ancona to Civitanova Marche (a distance of 27 miles);
B: Civitanova Marche to San Benedetto (25 miles);
C: San Benedetto to Pescara (40 miles);
D: Pescara to the south.

Simonds told Symes that in each of the four areas he wanted the 2SAS to insert by parachute, round up as many POWs as possible and then shepherd them to the coast, where another party of 2SAS would organize their extraction by boat.

The 1st Airborne Division had the task of organizing the insertion of the SAS party by parachute, while three SOE officers would oversee the seaborne embarkation and disembarkation from fishing boats.

Symes assigned to each area a 2SAS team comprised of seven soldiers. Responsible for Area A was Sergeant Major Bill Marshall, while Captain Peter Power was given B, Lieutenant Grant Hibbert had C and D was under Captain Simon Baillie. The latter was the largest area in geographical size, so two other parties – under the command of Lieutenant Alistair McGregor and Lieutenant Raymond Lee – would also insert into Area D to search for POWs.

Symes assembled the officers and men for Operation *Jonquil* in Bari on 1 October, and the next day they were briefed on the mission. At one minute before midnight on 2 October, the parties of Captain Power and Lieutenant McGregor, together with three SOE officers, sailed from Bari in eight fishing schooners. A few hours later, four Albemarle aircraft took off from Bari aerodrome containing the parachute teams for the four operational areas.

Symes and B Squadron sailed to Termoli, arriving just as the Germans launched their counter-attack on the afternoon of 4 October. While his men were drafted in to defend the town along the railway line, Symes sailed out of the port and headed north to check with Captain Baillie – who had left a day earlier – that *Jonquil* was underway. He returned on 6 October, the German counter-attack having failed, and announced that B Squadron would sail north, not in the caiques as originally planned but in LCIs.

Photographed in 2022, the harbour at Termoli was where 2SAS were attacked by Nazi aircraft on October 5, resulting in the death of Arthur Dench.

At 1800 hours that evening, the parties commanded by Lieutenant Hibbert, Captain Power and Sergeant Major Marshall sailed out of Termoli.

Marshall and Power's parties (A and B respectively) were landed at Grottammare, 100 miles north of Termoli, and Hibbert, leading C, came ashore a few miles south, just north of the mouth of the River Tronto. Both landing places were wide of the mark.[12] Nonetheless, Captain Baillie heard the sound of engines as the LCIs passed the landing beach, but despite repeated signals they were unable to contact the vessels, a failure that Baillie described as 'remarkable'.

Power walked his two parties inland until dawn. The rain was torrential and remained so throughout the next day. Having deduced they had been landed too far south, Power carried out a brief reconnaissance and then led his men north to the proper RV (rendezvous). On the night of 9/10 October, they signalled ashore a naval dinghy laden with supplies. There was also a message 'that the ship would not call again until the nights of October 24/25 and 25/26 owing to the moon, and that all prisoners must be embarked on these nights'.

---

12. Hibbert's party were so far out of position they were evacuated on 13 October.

B Squadron had been handed a formidable challenge. Deep inside Nazi territory, without any wireless sets – despite repeated requests, none had been provided – they had no means of extraction for a fortnight.

Power was not the sort of officer to be cowed. He subdivided his force into four: he would lead No1 party north to contact prisoners; No2 party, under the charge of Corporal Hughes, would go in a circle south and west; No3 would circle west and north; and No4, commanded by Sergeant Major Marshall, would remain on the river to receive prisoners and conduct a sweep of the coastal area for any other escapees. No3 party was the exception in that it comprised three privates, the most senior in age being Edwin Weaver, a handsome 37-year former artilleryman with an Errol Flynn moustache.

Power set off on 10 October, accompanied by Private Bob Tong and an American, Sergeant Joe Marino, a member of the Office of Strategic Services (OSS), the equivalent of the British SOE.[13]

Power kept a daily tally of their accomplishments in his log:

'11th Oct: Contacted 14 prisoners in the evening, including two South African officers.

'12th Oct: 4 British officers arrived at 11.00 hrs and told us there were a number of prisoners near Corridonia.

'13th Oct: Contacted another five or six prisoners.

'14th Oct: Arrived Corridonia area. Contacted one prisoner, who knew of 30 more.

'15th Oct: Contacted 9 more prisoners.

'16th Oct: Contacted a communist who was hiding about thirty prisoners. Searched up the river immediately south of Macerata.

'17th Oct: Found four prisoners. We all set out to return to the rendezvous.

'18th Oct: Contacted five or six prisoners west of Ferno.

'19th Oct: Contacted two prisoners.'

---

13. OSS worked with A Force in endeavouring to collect escaped POWs in Italy in a mission they codenamed *Simcol*. Of the fifteen personnel assigned to *Simcol*, five were attached to various SAS operations.

Power's party reached the coast on the later afternoon of 19 October. The next morning he left the POWs under the supervision of Tong and Marino and walked to Marshall's camp, where he found a further thirty-four POWs who had been retrieved by Marshall and his men over the last week. 'All going well,' noted Power in his journal.

However, their luck changed the next morning when a German patrol came up the river valley and spotted Marshall's base camp. Power wrote:

> 'Cook, who was doing sentry on the river, taken prisoner at 0630 hours. SSM Marshall, warned by Italians, came to the rescue, and shot the German who was guarding Cook. Cook escaped, but was subsequently recaptured. Fitzgerald taken prisoner … . Tong went down the river at 0700 hours to take over the guard from Cook, and ran into a German patrol, who threw a grenade at him. Escaped, and came to warn us. We lay up for the rest of the day in a ravine.'

Marshall was subsequently awarded a Military Medal for his conduct, the citation describing his actions:

> 'As he went down the path SSM Marshall was confronted by a German with two revolvers. He continued to advance until he was two yards from the German, who started to back away. At this moment SSM Marshall observed one of his own men who was disarmed and a prisoner. SSM Marshall thereupon shot the German with his TSMG [Thompson submachine gun], realizing that there were others about and enabling his own man to make a bolt for safety. A few minutes later SSM Marshall saw another of his own men being approached by the Germans, whom he shot at, wounding or hitting at least one. SSM Marshall showed great gallantry in engaging single-handed a German patrol of 16 strong, and his leadership of the party was of a very high order.'

The Germans evidently assumed they had encountered a group of stray POWs, rather than an organized search and rescue party inserted behind

Bob Tong, seen here on a return to Italy in 2012, was a young but effective member of Operation Jonquil.

enemy lines. There was no follow-up operation from the Germans, and over the course of the next forty-eight hours other SAS parties from the three operational areas began arriving with retrieved POWs. In total, noted Power, by the morning of the 24th there were 'about three or four hundred prisoners'.

The boat was scheduled to arrive at half past midnight on 25 October, and the instructions issued by Power to the prisoners was to 'come in parties not larger than three'. Power and Tong started towards the beach just before midnight in order to signal in the boat before bringing up the POWs. But as they neared the pick-up point, they heard gunshots. Power recorded what happened next in his log: '23:59 hours. Lorries arrived at German post, and patrolled road with headlights on. Sounds of prisoners stampeding back upstream. Decided it was foolish to signal boat in, beach being only 300 yards from road in German post, and absolutely flat and exposed.'

Power and Tong fled north, believing the operation had been fatally compromised. But the next evening, a Royal Navy launch arrived at the beach, where Bill Marshall embarked twenty-three prisoners without incident. The rest of the 400 or so who had been corralled by the SAS had decided to strike out south on foot. Not many reached the Allied lines.

It was another month before Power and Tong, together with five POWs they had picked up, returned to Allied lines, arriving at Termoli in a fishing boat piloted by an Italian aviation officer.

Power's experience became a familiar failing of Operation *Jonquil*. Inserting behind enemy lines wasn't the problem, nor was rounding up the POWs (although some prisoners believed anyone in uniform, whatever its colour, was not to be trusted); the challenge was in the extraction. One of the American OSS officers involved in the operation, Lieutenant Pete Sauro, parachuted into Italy with a small team and collected 250 fugitives within twenty-four hours. The Americans instructed the POWs to muster on the coast at Francavilla, approximately 20 miles due east from Sauro's operational base. A naval vessel

Just 20 in 1943, Bob Tong was a valued and resolute member of Operation Jonquil.

would arrive on the nights of 4, 6, 8 and 10 October between midnight and 0100 hours, and flash a light every fifteen minutes. 'Jack London' was the password.

More POWs were directed toward Francavilla by three other SAS parties scouring the countryside west and south of Pescara. In total, 600 had arrived on the coast: 350 British, 200 Yugoslav and fifty Americans.

It was now that the SAS men cursed their lack of radio communication, which had on many occasions been requested but to no avail. 'They had signalled for four nights (October 4, 6, 8 and 10), without success,' recorded the *Jonquil* report. 'On the fourth night (10th) what was believed to have been a German MTB [Motor Torpedo Boat] switched its searchlight on them, and there was an exchange of fire. At the same time a truckload of German troops arrived on the coast road above them.'

The demoralized POWS were told that the Royal Navy was not coming to their rescue; they would have to make their own way south to Termoli, 75 miles distant.

Peter Power, far left, front, and Jim Mackie, far right rear, were outstanding 2SAS officers.

On 14 October, Lieutenant Grant Hibbert and his party from Area C arrived at a coastal rendezvous point with thirty POWs. 'They signalled every night without success,' recorded the *Jonquil* report. 'Finally, after the area had been thoroughly combed, and they were certain that no POWs remained, they succeeded in bribing an Italian fisherman to mend his boat, and bring them back.'

Symes had landed with a party of seven men on the night of 15/16 October at a stretch of coastline approximately 45 miles north of Termoli. He sent patrols inland towards Chieti (west) and Casoli (south-west), and within six days the SAS had collected thirty POWs. The rendezvous had been prearranged for the night of 22/23 October, but Symes had just started to signal the boat when two Germans approached and the pick-up was aborted. He tried again two nights later, but there was no response to his

Lewis pressed himself on the floor as the hull of the MTB was shredded by enemy fire. Upon its cessation, he staggered onto deck, stepping over the bodies of at least six dead Italian sailors. 'Flames were licking along the railing,' said Lewis. 'From out in the blackness I could hear the desperate appeal of the Italian sailors who had jumped overboard with their life belts and were floating about crying for help.'

Raymond Lee was already in the water, nursing a wound to his shoulder, but confident he could swim the mile to shore. The Frenchman made it, and had the good fortune to be spotted by the A Force beach party who had avoided detection by the Germans. Lewis also reached land, whereupon he collapsed on the sand and 'watched, exhaustedly, [as] the fire on board reached the torpedo and the boat blew up'.

With the help of A Force, Lee was back at the 2SAS Termoli headquarters on 12 November, where he reported the death of everyone else aboard the MTB. Six weeks later, Captain Lewis appeared, having relied on the generosity of 'kind and unquestioning Italian peasants' as he trekked south. He would have reached Allied lines sooner had he not stumbled onto the front line of the 'long, drawn-out battle of the Sangro River'.

Though Termoli had been secured on 6 October, the advance of the British Eighth Army up the east coast of Italy then turned into a bloody slog. They finally crossed the Sangro (32 miles north of Termoli) on 23 November, but it required another five weeks of hard fighting before the 1st Canadian Infantry Division captured the deep-water port of Ortona.

Lieutenant Colonel Simonds estimated that about 900 escaped POWs had successfully emulated Lewis by reaching the Allied lines. Some had benefited from the assistance of A Force, but others had used their own initiative. It was a disappointing tally considering that an estimated 30,000 prisoners had walked out of their camps in Italy in September.

At the end of 1943, there was still one 2SAS unit deployed on Operation *Jonquil*, the seven-strong party command by Lieutenant Alastair McGregor, which had parachuted into the area on 2 October. Captain Simon Baillie had met McGregor at Villa Celiera (20 miles inland from Pescara) on 15 October, but he had since been incommunicado. One report had reached 2SAS HQ to the effect that McGregor and his men were active in the Gran Sasso region of central Italy with some Yugoslav partisans, but another rumour claimed that the seven SAS soldiers had been caught and executed by the Germans in the Chieti area.

McGregor, a pugnacious and audacious officer, was still very much alive as 1944 dawned. Having collected as many prisoners as he could in October, and delivered them to Baillie, McGregor then led his men on a guerrilla campaign, which was subsequently christened Operation *Begonia*. They ambushed enemy traffic on the roads, and hunted and executed fascist informers, taking their ill-gotten gains such as cars, money, black market food and clothes, and distributing them to the indigent locals. They were nearly caught on 5 January 1944, but the 2SAS men were always one step ahead of the Nazis and they managed to slip away from the encirclement of their hideout. It was another three weeks before McGregor and his men returned from the dead, landing in a boat they had bought for 100,000 lira at Fossacesia, midway between Pescara and Termoli to the south. The first soldiers they met were Canadians.

Lieutenant Colonel Bill Stirling highlighted several reasons for the ineffectiveness of Operation *Jonquil*, including the 'extremely erratic' timekeeping of the Royal Navy. But his chief criticism was that 'signalling arrangements were not satisfactory'. He added: 'Walkie-Talkies between shore and ship might have been useful. Wireless communications with the base would have prevented the ignorance of the parties of the amended orders issued.'

What frustrated Stirling most was the missed opportunity: 'Nevertheless given a simple plan with a reliable means of communication, and RVs, which could be depended on, it might have produced more satisfactory results.'

Chapter Ten

Captain Roy Farran and his men of D Squadron were withdrawn from Termoli in mid-October, moving into billets just outside Taranto, where they had landed six weeks earlier. 'All Southern Italy was at peace and we were very happy,' said Farran. It was the first respite the men had enjoyed since 10 September, and they made the most of it, visiting Taranto or driving further afield to Bari. But the lull was short-lived. Major Esmond Baring, 2SAS's representative at Eighth Army HQ, arrived one morning to brief Farran about a new operation. It was, in 2SAS tradition, codenamed after a flowering plant – *Candytuft* – and its objective was: 'To land by sea on the coast between Ancona and Pescara and attempt to derail a train near a curve on the coast railway.'

Extraction would be by naval craft which would rendezvous off the mouth of the River Tordino just south of the town of Giulianova on the first four nights in November, waiting to come inshore on a signal from Farran.

Farran organized the raiders into four parties of four men, three from his D Squadron and one from B Squadron, under the command of Lieutenant Grant Hibbert. He and Hibbert were the only officers among the sixteen saboteurs.

Having assembled his men, Farran explained the mission. They would all land on a stretch of coast approximately 35 miles north of Pescara at 2200 hours on 27 October. Splitting into their four parties, the raiders would head inland for 5 miles and lie up until the following night, when they would rendezvous at a track junction. Farran's party would attempt to derail a train by 0200 hours on 29 October. If they failed they would try again the following night, and again on the evening of 30/31 October.

Farran recalled:

> 'As soon as the train had been derailed, a party would blow large gaps in the line on either side of the train, and one party

would mine the main coast road. Telephone communications would also be cut. If no success had been achieved by the night 31 October/1st November, all parties would demolish the railway and mine the road regardless of trains. After the demolition had been completed all parties would make their way southwards to hide out … they would then make their way, by night, to the embarkation point.'

Farran's party returned to Termoli, where they embarked on an Italian MTB on the night of 27 October. The voyage to the drop-off point was uneventful, but as they glided towards the mouth of the River Tronto the skipper of the MTB spotted a dark shape up ahead. He ordered the engines cut. Farran asked what he had seen. 'A submarine charging its batteries,' the skipper whispered. 'I don't think they have seen us.' The skipper decided to risk going in, confident they would not be detected by the submarine. 'My nerves were so tensed that I could barely speak,' said Farran.

After several agonizing minutes, the MTB skipper gave Farran the all-clear and the crew of the vessel began to inflate the rubber dinghies. The SAS men climbed in and pushed off. 'There was only the sound of the paddles and the patter of the rain in the stillness of the night,' remembered Farran. 'I kept one eye on the submarine and the other on the sandy beach ahead. Never have I known a night so black.'

Farran's party reached the shore unseen, as did the other three dinghies, and the sixteen SAS men moved inland along the southern bank of the Tronto. It was raining heavily and their progress was impeded by the mud, but eventually they reached firmer ground and shortly before dawn Farran's section was ensconced in a thicket: 'There we lay, four miserable, half drowned men, shivering in our wet clothes under the bushes.'

The men dozed during the daylight hours, grateful that the rain had ceased but anxious for the return of night. When darkness came, they emerged from the bushes and headed for the rendezvous at the track junction. Lieutenant Hibbert and Sergeant Andrew Seddon were already there, braving the pouring rain, with their parties when Farran arrived, but there was no sign of the fourth stick, led by Sergeant Rawes. They couldn't wait. Farran recalled that 'in view of the low state of morale it was decided that nothing could be done that night. No trains had been observed on either night, so it was decided that all parties hide up in farms the next day, drying their clothes, and preparing fuses for a big demolition on the next night.'

Farran took his party west, and after a mile or so they spotted at dilapidated cottage set back from the track. 'It is an infallible rule that if one is seeking shelter, the poorest dwellings will always give refuge,' commented Farran. 'Rich houses are unreliable.'

The cottage was inhabited by an elderly peasant couple, as kind-hearted as they were poor. They rekindled their dying fire and the old woman cooked a chicken, frying it with some tomatoes. The bedraggled SAS troops had never enjoyed a meal more. Farran and his men slept well that night, warm and dry, and they woke in the morning reinvigorated. They spent the day preparing their charges for the raid that evening and then sat down to another hearty meal. 'I think they guessed what we were about to do because the old man warned me about the sentries on the bridge,' Farran remembered. 'His wife clasped our wrists in both her hands and cried as she kissed us all.'

L/Cpl Leslie Bennett was one of the men who lost their lives on Operation Maple Driftwood. His body was never recovered and he is commemorated on the Casino Memorial.

The three sticks rendezvoused without incident, but there was still no sign of Sergeant Rawes' party. Farran and Hibbert would target different stretches of the railway line, and Seddon and his three men would mine the road and knock out telegraph poles. They agreed to use thirty-minute fuses timed to explode at 2330 hours.

By the time Farran's party had reached the railway line, the wind had got up and it was driving the rain into their faces. It was a foul night, but one likely to keep all but the most stout-hearted sentry under cover. The SAS force worked with speed and efficiency, laying the charges and then withdrawing down the embankment and across some fields. 'We heard the sound of explosions

MAPLE • PARTY

Sgt BENSON • 4121828 •

Sergeant Robert Benson is believed to have been executed by the Germans during Operation Maple Driftwood He has no known grave and is listed on the Casino Memorial.

and saw the flashes through the rain,' remembered Farran. Nevertheless, the men did not hang about congratulating one another. There was no time to waste, as there would now be enemy soldiers looking for them. The terrain was treacherous and it took them more than four hours to cover 10 miles.

Farran's party took shelter in a farm, as did Hibbert's, but Seddon's stick was fired on by a German patrol. The men scattered, two going one way and two another. The explosions were heard by Sergeant Rawes and his stick, who had spent two days wandering the area trying to find the rendezvous party. Heartened by the realization that their compatriots had undertaken their task, Rawes and his men lay charges on a section of railway line, demolished two telegraph poles and mined a road.

On 2 November, they reached the rendezvous point, picking up two of Sergeant Seddon's stick along the way. Everyone was there. Farran led them to the beach, and at one minute to midnight he flashed the identification signal out to sea. Sixteen minutes later, an MTB hove into view, with Major Sandy Scratchley extending a cheerful greeting. Farran couldn't resist leaving a parting gift for the enemy: 'Charges were laid on telegraph poles and on the main road before we left, to go off in three days.'

Lieutenant Colonel Bill Stirling liked his officers to include in their operational reports an appendix about 'lessons learnt'; that was how a regime grew and evolved. Among the lessons that Farran had absorbed during Operation *Candytuft* was the need for gas capes and waterproof bags for fuses. He also explained why 'desert type commando boots are useless for this country': they had no grip on any slippery surface. He further wrote that when the weather was inclement, it was 'considered almost impracticable to hide up in the open except in the case of extreme emergency. All the farmers in the country away from the immediate vicinity of main roads and villages are extremely helpful.'

This was advice that Sandy Scratchley acted upon a few weeks later when he led a five-strong team

Bombardier Albert Pugh from London was another member of Operation Maple Driftwood whose fate has never been conclusively determined.

ashore on Operation *Sleepy Lad*, the first 2SAS mission not to be codenamed in honour of a flowering plant. The raiders were landed on 18 November just north of the River Musone, about 14 miles south of Ancona. With them they had an Italian guide, Luigi, specifically brought along to help liaise with locals. Remembering Farran's advice about farms, Scratchley's party tried the first farm they came to and received a royal welcome. They remained at the farm during the daytime of 19 November, making plans for that evening, and at nightfall two of the men, Corporal John McGuire and Private Selwyn Brown, were despatched to blow up the railway – preferably with a train as well – on the curve of the line north of Porto Recanati. Scratchley, Luigi and Private Josef

Irishman Austin Hehir, MM, seen here in his POW camp in 1945, proved his worth behind the lines on Operation Maple Thistledown.

went off to blow up the line north of Loreto and cut some telephone lines.

All the raiders were back at the farm on the night of 23/24 November, having accomplished their tasks, albeit without destroying a train. Scratchley also gathered some intelligence about German troop strength in the area, which he subsequently passed on to Eighth Army HQ. But when they reached the RV point there was no response to their signal; not on the first night or the three that followed. 'The failure to be picked up was therefore doubly annoying as ... I was in a hurry to return with the information,' remarked Scratchley in his report. Eventually they contacted a local partisan, Mariane Berushki, who moved them from the farm to a more secure location and arranged for a fishing boat to ferry them back to Allied lines. 'The people of the land, good honest and genuine,' wrote Scratchley in the conclusion to his report. He was less impressed by the Royal Navy, who in his estimation failed to pick them up because they were anchored off the wrong beach.

Bill Stirling did not like being dependent on the Royal Navy for his operations, and he continued to submit proposals for raids in which 2SAS would insert by parachute. This was, after all, the reason why the SAS had been raised in 1941. In December 1943, he pitched two operations to Eighth Army HQ, one codenamed *Pomegranate* and the other *Maple*. The objective of the first was to destroy German aircraft prior to the Allied landings at Anzio and Nettuno (Operation *Shingle*), and the aim of the second was to cut enemy rail communications in central Italy, hindering the Germans' ability to send reinforcements south to the beachheads. In both cases, Stirling argued that an amphibious landing would be impractical as it would involve a gruelling march across rough terrain to the target and also reduce the amount of explosives and other equipment that could be carried by the raiders.

Both operations got the go-ahead, but the weather intervened and they were postponed from their scheduled start date of 18 December. Operation *Maple* finally got underway three weeks later, on 7 January. It was sub-divided into two factions: *Maple Thistledown*, totalling seventeen men, and *Maple Driftwood*, comprising eight men under the command of Captain John Gunston, formerly of the Irish Guards and the son of the Unionist MP Sir Derrick Wellesley. The men

Another member of the ill-fated Operation Maple Driftwood: Sapper William Dodds, from Edinburgh.

of *Maple Thistledown* jumped from two Dakotas north-west of Aquila at Colla Futa, and Gunston's party parachuted onto a DZ north-west of Ancona. 'We landed successfully in about three feet of snow and had no difficulty in collecting the panniers which had been kicked out of the plane before the stick,' wrote Lieutenant David Worcester in his report. 'It was very cold – about 15 degrees Fahrenheit below zero.' Worcester and his four men rallied with the party led by Sergeant Major John Lloyd, although there was no sign of the

This photo, taken by Austin Hehir in his POW camp, is of some Polish inmates.

other two sticks. For three days the nine men marched towards the target area. Worcester continued: 'The party was very exhausted as our packs weighed about 45 pounds and the windproof suits which we wore over our battle dress over-burdened us with clothing. We obtained a meal at an Italian's house where we stayed the night.'

Worcester and Lloyd parted company, having agreed on their objectives, and the former continued marching for two more days. Along the way they were joined by three POWs, still on the run having escaped from their camp the previous September. Worcester established his headquarters close to a village, just north of the two roads from Greccio to Configni. They then went to work. Worcester and another soldier made a reconnaissance of the bridge at Orte, and when they returned to their HQ it was to learn that a sabotage party under Sergeant Smoker had derailed a train north of Terni, 20 miles north-east. Partisans soon heard of the SAS presence and flocked to their HQ, offering their services. 'They were under the leadership of an Italian major who offered us the use of an 88mm gun,' Worcester said in his report. There were seventy-two Italians in total, but most were not considered reliable.

When no trains were seen in the next week, Worcester made a decision: 'We broke up the 60lbs of charges intended for the railway and made them into bombs of about 1 pound each for use against road transport. Fortunately we had with us a large number of detonators and also two 1¼ pound thermite incendiary bombs per man.'

Roy Farran set himself and his men high standards, and once RTUd an officer for being 'weak, wet and windy'.

The SAS men then embarked on a series of ambushes on the Terni to Rome road. Among the attacks that stood out in Worcester's memory was one against a staff car as it travelled down the road. Private Austin Hehir, an Irishman from Lahinch in County Clare, 'drew his two revolvers and walked up the road firing at the car which was approaching at about 30 miles an hour. The car stopped and both its occupants were killed.' Hehir repeated his 'Wild West' feat a couple of days later, with the same result.

Over the course of ten days, the SAS force destroyed or damaged twenty-five vehicles during day and night attacks. Hehir's tactic was the

BUCKINGHAM PALACE.

I greatly regret that I am
unable to give you personally the
award which you have so well earned.
I now send it to you with
my congratulations and my best
wishes for your future happiness.

George R.I.

1595481 Gnr. A. Hehir, M.M.

The Royal Regiment of Artillery.

Austin Hehir received this letter from King George VI congratulating him on his Military Medal.

exception; in most cases, the damage was done by throwing their bombs at the back of the vehicles as they passed. The snow made the vehicles an easy target because they had to slow down to negotiate bends. 'There were only one or two trains every day and I decided against attacking the railway again as the results would not justify having to move from the otherwise good operational area in which we were,' wrote Worcester in his report.

The raiders continued to operate until their explosives ran out in early February, and then laid low until the end of the month, waiting for the weather to improve so they could extract. Worcester split his men into three groups, which included three Allied POWs who had joined their ranks, and then they parted. Worcester had with him Hehir and one of the POWS, a Lance Corporal Cobley, and they headed south towards Sora. 'We were very short of food but in spite of this we did some hard marching, covering about 25 miles a day (one day we covered 38 miles),' noted Worcester. The further south they marched, the more Germans they had to avoid. On the night of 3 March, they laid up near a village but in the early hours of the next morning were kicked awake by German jackboots. 'I was taken next door and asked for my papers, then stripped of everything worth taking,' said Worcester. They were treated fairly well, he said, and after a cursory interrogation, he, Hehir and Cobley were left in a room with five Germans guarding them. Worcester later reported:

'At about 0600 hours I noticed that the enemy, who were middle-aged, were becoming drowsy so I asked for some water. A bottle of wine and a glass were produced and I threw these at the first two Germans. We then made an attempt to escape. I was hit in my leg by Schmeisser fire early in the scrap and I saw Cobley go down in a corner with two Germans on top of him. Hehir was hit twice, first in the arm and then the leg, but kept fighting and eventually a German stood over him as he lay on the floor and emptied the whole magazine from the Schmeisser at him. Fortunately only four bullets hit him in the stomach. My leg was useless and I thought Hehir was dying. We were laid on the bed and I managed to give Hehir a shot of morphine which made him lose consciousness.'

Despite their wounds, the three British soldiers survived, spending several weeks in an Italian hospital before being transported to Germany and incarceration. Upon his repatriation, the indefatigable Austin Hehir received a Military Medal, the concluding paragraph of the citation for which stated:

'During his year's imprisonment, Pte Hehir did not cease to continue to display the same qualities of courage and initiative. On four different occasions he succeeded in escaping from various prison camps in Germany, but was always recaptured before he reached the frontier. On one of these occasions he was again wounded in the back. Finally, in April 1945 in spite of his ill-health, Hehir succeeded in escaping from Stalag 7 at Moosburg and reached an advanced American unit after a march of a fortnight. He obtained arms and continue to fight with this unit up to Linz until the Armistice. Pte Hehir's conduct both during and subsequent to this operation (Maple) showed a devotion to duty which never wavered.'

David Worcester's recompense for his conduct behind the lines was a Military Cross. The citation praised his 'indomitable courage, initiative and offensive spirit [which] inspired his men to carry on in the face of tremendous odds … . Lieutenant Worcester demonstrated how much can be accomplished by determined brave men, although they may be completely cut off from their own troops and faced with appalling geographical conditions.'. Throughout, added the citation, 'this tiny party of one officer and four men were a constant thorn in the side of the Germans'.

None of the twenty-five men on Operation *Maple* returned from the mission. Most were caught, such as Sergeant Major John Lloyd's party, which had assembled on the DZ with Worcester's stick. Lloyd was an inspiring and innovative leader, and his men sabotaged railway lines and ambushed Italian Carabinieri throughout January. On 1 February, he split his section and instructed them to make for the Allied lines. Lloyd made it to Rome and was sheltered by a resistance network until 22 April, when he set out to cross the front lines. On 24 April, he was within sight of the British forward positions in the middle of no man's land, where that evening he made contact with a British patrol. Lloyd thought he had made it, but within minutes the group ran into a German patrol and they were all taken prisoner.

Eight men of Operation Maple were never seen again. This was *Driftwood*, under the command of John Gunston. It was later reported that on 7 March, Captain Gunston, a skilled amateur sailor, had been seen with his men putting out to sea in a 22ft boat at Porto San Giorgio, 35 miles south of their operational area. 'No subsequent news has been received,' stated the *Maple* report. Their fate remains a mystery. It was a rough night when the boat was launched and they may have all drowned. However, not long after the end of the war, a German intelligence report was uncovered that described the capture of three men who had swum to the shore in central Italy after the foundering of their boat. They were questioned and then executed, and their bodies secretly buried. The names in the report were Captain John Gunston, Sergeant Robert Benson and Private Herbert Loosemore, all of whom had been on Operation *Maple*.

Maple produced mixed results. Several railway lines were cut and vehicles ambushed, but it had deprived 2SAS of twenty-five highly trained men. In the report on the operation, four reasons were stated for the high casualty rate:

1) The static conditions at Anzio which made it necessary for all SAS men to exfiltrate instead of being overrun.
2) The precautions which the Germans were taking to affect the recapture of escaped prisoners.
3) The winter conditions and lack of food in the area immediately north of the front line.
4) The tendency of some of the groups to stay too long in the same area instead of exfiltrating when their tasks were finished and supplies were running low.

Chapter Eleven

Like Operation *Maple*, the 2SAS mission codenamed *Pomegranate* had initially been scheduled for December 1943, but it was postponed because of the winter weather. By this time the regiment had installed themselves at Noci, a town halfway between Taranto and Bari. Their HQ was a villa on the outskirts of town and the officers' mess was on the other side of the road. Some of the 2SAS officers lived elsewhere in Noci because of overcrowding in the villa. One was Lieutenant Jimmy Hughes, who had joined the regiment in the summer, having served with the Royal Artillery during the siege of Malta.

The war had put Hughes' ambition of becoming an architect on hold, but during the training at Philippeville he had found a perverse pleasure from the demolitions course. 'Just as I derived a satisfaction from designing and building, so did I find equal satisfaction in destroying and demolishing, and there was a certain precision and cleanliness in the way in which it was now done,' he recalled.

Parachuting, on the other hand, was nothing but unalloyed terror, but Hughes nonetheless completed the training and was now waiting to become operational.

Throughout November and December 1943, the 2SAS men not deployed on operations trained hard in the countryside around Noci. 'I now had my own troop of four and we would go off for days learning to live off the land and to move silently and easily, both by day and by night,' said Hughes.

Christmas was a welcome respite from the training, and the officers' mess at Noci was decorated with balloons, paper chains and a tree. Quantities of wine and food were procured and a dance was held, to which many locals were invited. Hughes fell in a love with a young woman called Elizabetta, a wartime infatuation all too common among young men facing an uncertain future. 'I

Lt Jimmy Hughes survived horrific wounds and also evaded the Gestapo to return to England and warn the SAS of Hitler's Commando Order.

would carry a picture of Elizabetta in my mind as a sort of escape route from hard reality,' said Hughes. 'The image of her would give me the strength to resolve to return – with her there I would survive. Everyone needs a stronger reason then the mere thirst for life itself.'

Hughes learned of his selection for Operation *Pomegranate* early in January 1944. The officer in charge of the mission was Captain Antony Widdrington, 'a big man in every sense of the word', according to Hughes. Second in command was Hughes, and the rest of the unit comprised Lance Corporal John Malloy, Private 'Sweeney' Todd, Private Stanley McCormick and Private Tom Cox. In layman's terms, recalled Hughes, the purpose of Operation *Pomegranate* was to 'put out the eyes of the Germans so they would not see the preparations which were taking place for the seaborne attack on Anzio'.

This attack, codenamed Operation *Shingle*, involved the landing of two Allied divisions on beachheads at Anzio and Nettuno, around 30 miles south

*Jimmy Hughes,
bottom left, next to
his sergeant Ralph
'Jock' Hay, posing
for the camera
in Noci, Italy, in
December 1943.*

of Rome. it was hoped that the operation would outflank the Germans dug in on the Winter Line – the defensive fortification in western Italy focused on the town of Monte Cassino – and enable an assault on the Italian capital.

The 'eyes' referred to by Hughes were on the airfield at Sant Egidio, situated on a plain halfway between Assisi and Perugia. They were reconnaissance planes, Messerchmitt 410s and modified Junkers 88s. The RAF had unsuccessfully attempted to bomb the airfield, while a seaborne landing was considered impractical because of Sant Egidio's central location. Therefore, 'it was felt that here was an opportunity for the use of the 2nd SAS regiment'.

The Northwest African Photographic Reconnaissance Wing (NAPRW) constructed a large-scale model of the aerodrome and other intelligence details. Hughes recalled: 'We spent several hours in memorising every detail, the position of the hangers, the aircraft control tower, the line of the perimeter

Lt Jimmy Hughes, pictured, and Captain Antony Widdrington became separated from the rest of the men on Operation Pomegranate and proceeded alone to the target.

and the guard huts, so that we felt confident that, even if blindfolded, we could find our way around, for the attack had to take place in the dark.'

Captain Widdrington decided that instead of packing their equipment into the standard airborne cylindrical containers,[14] they would instead place everything inside 50-gallon oil drums because they would not have time to bury the containers; if the enemy came across abandoned oil drums, they might not connect them with enemy guerrilla activity.

---

14. The canisters were 5ft 6in long and 16in wide, and when full weighed approximately 100lb. A parachute pack was attached to one end, and they deployed in the standard way when pushed from the aircraft.

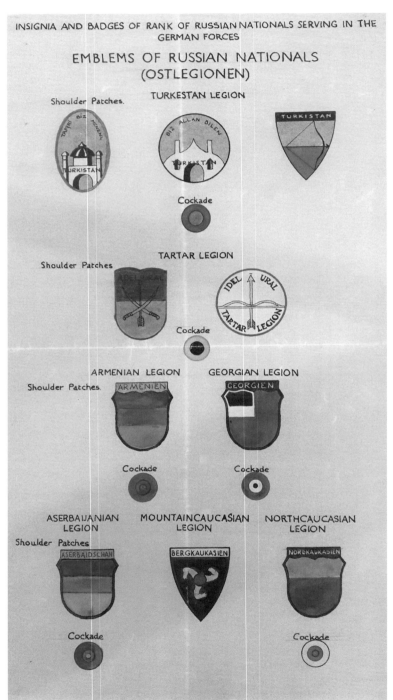

This fact sheet on enemy insignia was compiled by Jimmy Hughes prior to Operation Pomegranate.

The DZ selected for the operation was at a point east of Lake Trasimene, in the valley running eastwards near Magione.

Having been briefed about the operation, Hughes wrote letters to his parents and to Elizabetta, the first phlegmatic and the second passionate. Then he busied himself with final preparations, determined to keep anxiety at bay. Hughes reflected:

> 'Imagination is a strange characteristic of the human mind. In order to survive each man must learn how first to test it in order, in broad terms, to measure the odds, and then to switch it off lest it become an impediment in the execution of a task. Free ranging imagination was unsupportable. I must think of other things.'

He dyed all their webbing belts dark brown, stripped, cleaned and reassembled his American carbine and .45 Colt automatic, and packed the explosives. These were Lewes bombs, invented in 1941 by Lieutenant Jock Lewes, a founding member of the SAS. They were a lump of plastic explosive and thermite rolled in motor car oil, to which was added a No27 detonator, an instantaneous fuse and a time pencil. The time pencil was similar in shape and size to a pen. It was a glass tube with a spring-loaded striker held in place by a strip of copper wire. At the top was a glass phial containing acid which one squeezed gently to break. The acid would then eat through the wire and release the striker. The thicker the wire, the longer the delay before the striker was triggered.

Before leaving base, Widdrington and Hughes had consulted Lieutenant 'Dusty' Miller, the Royal Engineers officer on secondment to 2SAS as their explosives expert. Widdrington said that he wanted to carry the bombs and igniter sets under his parachute harness, so Miller advised him to use lead delays instead of time pencils as these were more robust than the latter. Miller explained how the lead delay fired the charge and how their timings were dependent on the temperature. Hughes recalled:

> 'We chose a delay which, at 65 degrees Fahrenheit (18 degrees centigrade) would explode our charges in one hour knowing that, during the attack, the temperature would drop to not much above freezing point and this should slow down the mechanism and give

us two hours before the explosion would take place from the time
we primed the igniter sets.'

Normal procedure when assembling the igniter sets was to crimp a detonator
onto the end of the lead delay, with another detonator (with thirty seconds of
fuse and a pull lighter) fastened to the first detonator. In this way, if the raiders
were discovered planting the bombs, they could pull the igniter and throw the
bomb at the plane or the enemy soldiers.

The hours of 12 January ticked by slowly for Hughes and his five
comrades. They were primed to depart that evening, but only if the weather
was satisfactory. At 1600 hours, they learned that the forecast was good and
the operation was on. They boarded a truck and were driven to a USAAF
base at Gioia, where they were introduced to the crew of the DC3 aircraft of
No38 Troop Carrier Wing and given a short briefing. The 2SAS party had
something to eat and at 2000 hours they were instructed to board the DC3.
'There was that usual feeling of tenseness, a light tightening of the muscles
around the chest which I always felt at the moment of take-off and then we
were airborne,' said Hughes. The aircraft flew north-west over Foggia, west of
Aquila and then to Lake Trasimene. First out of the aircraft would be the two
oil drums, then Hughes, and last to leave would be Widdrington. The aircraft
descended to 500ft, and with the help of two American aircrew, Hughes heaved
out the drums. He followed: 'I was out in the icy cold air of a January Italian
night, a few moments of inert suspension and all was black.' His landing was
the gentlest he had experienced. 'I slapped the release pad and eased myself
out of the harness. The ground was soft and furrowed by the plough, all around
was stillness, and I began to shiver.'[15]

Hughes's five comrades also made perfect landings and the two oil drums
were swiftly located. The omens looked good for Operation *Pomegranate*.
They were soon climbing a hill away from the DZ, and as dawn began to
break they concealed themselves among dense foliage. Widdrington and three
men bedded down in one area, Hughes and Lance Corporal Malloy in another.
'[We] found a suitable bush, unrolled our brown sleeping bags and were soon

---

15. The aircraft that dropped Hughes and his comrades failed to return to base, its
wreckage later being located on the slopes of Monte Tezio, a few miles east of the
DZ. It was believed the DC3 crashed into the mountainside in poor visibility.

fast asleep,' recalled Hughes. 'During the long day we dozed and dreamed and spoke no word to each other, waiting for the dusk.'

When Widdrington appeared at nightfall, he brought troubling news. During the day, some local woodsmen had chanced upon their hiding place; that wasn't in itself alarming. They could be trusted. But they told the British soldiers that the Germans had arrived at the drop zone at dawn and were now actively hunting the parachutists. Widdrington and Hughes agreed that even the Germans, who had a reputation for being unimaginative, would probably be able to deduce that if a small party of enemy soldiers had dropped into the area, their likely target would be Sant Egidio airfield.

There was nothing they could do but press on, marching as rapidly as they could during the hours of darkness. Hughes remembered:

> 'The ground was steep with shale and the crevices were filled with snow, but with our thick clothes and heavy loads we were hot and sticky, and shirts stuck to sweaty bodies. From time to time we stopped to rest and each of us scooped a handful of cold snow and held it to his mouth.'

The party had one Bren gun, the carrying of which was shared between Hughes and Malloy.

They marched for seven hours the following night, but the thick mud sapped the stamina from their legs. They continued the pattern of laying up during the day and moving at night, and spent most of 14 January on top of Monte Tuzzio near an old well. Their reward was a brew, using water from a pool that clearly was also a source for cows, which Hughes said they nevertheless appreciated:

> 'Someone took a mess-tin and filled it with the muddy water of the pool, dropping in the two sterilisation tablets. Another collected brushwood and a third climbed down into the dark hole. Soon we had a little fire going, burning brightly at the bottom of the empty well, throwing upwards a cone of light invisible to the surroundings. And so we had our first and last cup of tea, and it tasted good.'

Invigorated, the six men set off towards the River Tiber. 'When we reached it we found the river in spate and not fordable,' remarked Hughes. This was a blow, and they cursed the intelligence reports that had confidently asserted the river was not in full flow. Widdrington took the plunge, literally, followed by Hughes. 'We both began to wade out, but soon the water was up to our knees though we had hardly started the crossing,' said Hughes. They turned back to the bank and decided to try further down river.

By a stroke of good fortune, they came across an overhead rope cable-way a couple of hundred yards downriver. On their side, the cable ran out from a little brick hut, across the river, to the terminus on the far bank. 'It was a hand-operated device, never devised for a secret crossing,' reflected Hughes. Widdrington ordered two soldiers into the rudimentary chairs, constructed like those on a ski lift. 'The chair rattled and the cables thrummed through the quiet night as you went across two by two,' said Hughes. It required four trips in total to get the six men and their equipment across. Suddenly there was a curse, as Lance Corporal Malloy realized he had left his carbine on the other bank. They could not risk leaving the weapon, not with Germans looking for them, so Malloy was winched back with Widdrington's admonition wringing in his ears. When he returned with his carbine, the six men set off, but almost immediately a challenge was barked: '*Halt! Wer da?*'

Everyone froze for what seemed an age. Hughes said that Widdrington then gave the order to disperse:

> 'Unfortunately the direction which he and I took led to a cul-de-sac. We turned round and went the same way as I thought the others had gone, but we were unable to find them. We walked on, stopping to whistle at intervals, but we neither heard nor saw anyone. After three quarters of an hour we gave up hope of contacting the remainder of the party again. We crossed the railway and the main road and made eastwards into the hills.'[16]

Widdrington and Hughes walked until 0400 hours on 15 January. It was hard for Hughes, not a natural athlete, to keep pace with the taller and more powerful

---

16. In the operational report, written by Hughes a few months later, he said that the four carried on towards the target but aborted the raid upon discovering Widdrington and Hughes had beaten them to the airfield. They returned safely. Post-war, Hughes said the four were RTU'd by Bill Stirling after they gave inconsistent accounts of their movements after becoming separated from their two officers.

to find any more aircraft to attack. We sat down and began to disarm the remaining bombs. I had finished my work and was about four yards away from Major Widdrington.'

Suddenly there was a thunderous explosion. Hughes was hurled through the air, his trousers ripped from his legs in flight. He hit the ground, dazed and blinded. Hughes located Widdrington by his moaning: 'He had lost both hands and was badly wounded in the right leg and in the chest. I found my morphia syringe but dropped the piercing pin and as I was blind I could not find it.'

Showing remarkable presence of mind, given his injuries, Hughes rifled through his pockets, and those of Widdrington, pulling out whatever papers and maps he could find. Still unable to see, he piled up the papers and then, fumbling with a box of matches, managed to set them alight. By the time German guards arrived, Captain Widdrington was dead.[17]

Hughes was taken to a dressing station and then transferred to hospital in Perugia. Though a German intelligence officer told Hughes that only one aircraft had been destroyed, he learned later from an Italian working in the hospital that the actual tally was seven. The same German informed Hughes that he was under instructions from the Gestapo to hand his prisoner over for execution as soon as possible. 'As authority for this they quoted an order alleged to have been issued by the Fuhrer's HQ in December 1942, which stated that all saboteurs, whether wearing uniform or civilian clothes, would be shot,' recounted Hughes.

In the room next to Hughes was Major Gerhard Schacht, a distinguished paratrooper officer in the elite 1st Fallschirmjager Division. Schacht had been part of the assault force that had seized the Belgian fort of Eben-Emael in an audacious operation in May 1940, and had subsequently been appointed to the staff of General Kurt Student, the commander of the Fallschirmjager.

Schacht, opposed to Hitler's Commando Order on principle, used his influence with the chief doctor in the hospital, Hans-Gunther Sontgerath, to

---

17. Furnished by Hughes with the details of what had happened, Captain 'Dusty' Miller surmised that because Widdrington had carried his remaining bombs in his hand, or close to his body, he had inadvertently warmed them up. This reduced the timing of the lead delay, so the bombs exploded after an hour and twenty minutes instead of the two hours that they had anticipated.

tell the Gestapo that Hughes was too ill to be moved. Schact also organized an eminent Italian eye specialist, Professor Filippo Caramazza, to operate on Hughes's right eye, which resulted in the sight being saved. It was now six weeks since Hughes had arrived at the hospital, during which time Schacht had been released. Nonetheless, he kept abreast of the situation and, noted Hughes in his account of his period in captivity, used his influence once more on 4 March:

> 'Major Schacht telephoned to the doctor to say that the Secret Police had renewed their demands for me to be handed over for execution. Major Schacht went at once to General Kesselring's HQ and arranged with the G1 [staff officer responsible for personnel and administration] to reword the report so that I should not be classed as a saboteur. It was arranged that I should be sent by a hospital train via Padua to a Luftwaffe camp in Germany to avoid the prisoner of war collecting centre at Verona, where it would be likely that I would be subjected to further interrogation. They considered that once I had arrived at a prisoner of war camp in Germany I would be safe from any further trouble.'

Thanks to Schact's intervention, Hughes's status on his POW file was reworded from 'Political Prisoner' to 'Prisoner of War'. This enabled Dr Sontgerath to move the Englishman from the hospital, and on 10 March he was sent by train to Florence, where he was admitted to another prisoner hospital. Hughes immediately began plotting his escape; a drainpipe outside his window was one possibility, but that evening he and the other inmates were put on a train to Padua.

'We were warned that machine guns were placed pointing down the train, that sentries would patrol the platform in front of our carriage at every station, and that all tunnels, bridges and stations would be guarded by night,' wrote Hughes.

He took the warning lightly. So, too, did a British signaller called Bill Taylor and an American airman, Jess Bradburn, a waist gunner in a B24 who had been shot down the previous month. In the early hours of 11 March, not long after the train had left Modena, Hughes said the trio leapt from the train: 'We started walking and passed round the north of Modena and crossed the railway line from Modena to Bologna 50 yards west of the river bridge guarded by a German sentry. We came to a farmhouse where we got civilian clothes and were well fed.'

For the next week, the three men trekked in a south-easterly direction, tramping over hills that ran parallel to the Bologna to Rimini road. On 19 March, they were directed to a priest at San Valentino, who had contacts with the local partisans. The priest explained to the fugitives how to reach their remote headquarters. 'This involved climbing into the high ground,' said Hughes. 'There was a heavy snow storm and we had to make our way through the snow.' The locals they encountered on their trek were suspicious of the three and refused to give any information about the partisans. It was not until 22 March that they finally reached the partisans' headquarters. Taylor and Bradburn had been carrying slight wounds and needed a period of recuperation. Not Hughes; he was anxious to get back to England with the information about Hitler's Commando Order.

Hughes was first flown to Caserta, where he endured an interview with a 'pompous little staff officer' from 15th Army Group. He had made a note of the German units he had seen on the road following his escape from the train, but the staff officer didn't believe the information. 'To say the least, I felt annoyed,' said Hughes. 'I was the one who had crouched by the side of the road for hours, noting the units and counting the vehicles as they passed down to the front line. What made him think he knew better?'

Hughes was back with 2SAS in early May 1944 and was immediately debriefed by Major Eric Barkworth, the regiment's intelligence officer. This experience was 'much more serious and considered'. Barkworth was sufficiently alarmed by what he heard to submit a top secret report to 21st Army Group entitled 'The Hughes Case'. The report was greeted with a mix of scepticism and anxiety. Concerned that knowledge of the Nazis' Commando Order might spread fear and alarm among British soldiers, 21st Army Group duly shelved 'The Hughes Case'. His experience was dismissed as 'a mere German interrogation technique', but Major Barkworth raised objections. He pointed to the number of 2SAS men who remained unaccounted for after disappearing during operations in Italy, but he was told that that this could be 'explained away by the fact that the enemy probably wished to keep us in the dark about the success of the operation'.

Chapter Twelve

Private Cyril Wheeler volunteered for 2SAS in the summer of 1943. He had endured a hard life, born into poverty in Portsmouth and eventually put into a Barnardo's care home by his single mother. He trained to be a boot repair boy and, like so many other young men of his class, the outbreak of war in 1939 offered an opportunity for adventure. He enlisted in the Royal Engineers and was sent to France with the British Expeditionary Force. Wheeler was one of the fortunate sappers to successfully evacuate from Dunkirk.

His battalion was subsequently sent to North Africa, where they dug too many slit trenches for Wheeler's liking: 'It was in Algiers that the SAS came up. I think about 30 of us volunteered. They just came and started talking to men, and no one knew what it was. I thought it was a good chance to get out of the transit camp, [as] I was getting bored.'

The training at Philippeville was varied and demanding, he remembered: 'We did map reading, field craft, explosives, swimming; we were up at 6am and we never had 5 minutes breather.'

Parachute training was the only part of training that Wheeler found disagreeable: 'We had a railway bogey with four wheels, and we pushed that up the top of a rise. Then we sat on sides and came down, jumping out of the back and rolling. There were a lot of serious injuries doing that.'

Worse was to come when Wheeler and his fellow recruits moved onto the parachuting proper at an instruction centre outside Algiers. 'We were waiting down on the DZ and we saw the first lot come out,' he recalled. 'The second man's chute didn't open and he really banged down. We thought we wouldn't have to do it, but we did and that was my first jump.'

Wheeler's first operation with 2SAS was also the regiment's last hurrah in Italy in the winter of 1943/44. To the relief of Wheeler, it didn't involve leaping out of an aircraft.

Operation *Baobab* (named after a tree that is native to tropical Africa) was led by Captain Peter Power, and among the officers included in the raiding party were Lieutenants Douglas Laws and Grant Hibbert, the latter one of the most experienced soldiers in 2SAS. 'Hibbert was a very tall thin man with glasses, younger than me,' remembered Wheeler. 'He was strict and upright, a good officer, respected. You had to get on with your officers as they did with us.'

The target was a railway bridge 4 miles north of Fano on the coastal line between Ancona and Rimini. Lieutenant Colonel Bill Stirling arranged for aerial reconnaissance photos of the bridge by the NAPRW, and, as with Operation *Pomegranate*, a scale model was built of the target. Having studied the bridge as a model, Power and his men underwent several dress rehearsals.

'For the Italy raid we did a lot of practice runs,' remembered Wheeler. 'We commandeered this four-mast schooner and went up the coast with our Italian crew and our canoes. We went off the back of the schooner and practised paddling in to shore, to Molfetta harbour.'

It was Molfetta, just north of Bari, where Lieutenant Laws and a signaller called Buchan Dowell departed early in the afternoon of 29 January 29 in a motor schooner. Their destination was a stretch of coastline 300 miles north. The intention was to set the pair down just south of Pesaro, but because of thick fog they landed to the north, paddling ashore in a canoe and climbing a cliff face before finding a suitable place of concealment in a cave. The operational report stated:

> 'At 0800 hours on the 30th of January, Lieutenant Laws signalled by wireless that he had landed. The signal was received. Subsequently he made a reconnaissance in daylight. Moving across country to the south of Pesaro he noticed a body of nine Germans who were marching down the road from Pesaro to Fano. At 1400 hours he sent a signal that the area was patrolled and that the landing should not be made before 2300 hours; he returned to the cave for the rest of the day. At 1800 hours he left the cave and arrived at the bridge at 2300 hours.'

At 2315 hours, Laws signalled out to sea. Captain Power and the raiding party had been waiting off shore for an hour, pacing the deck of the destroyer

Bari on Italy's eastern coast, seen here in 2022, was where B Squadron, 2SAS, based themselves in September 1943.

HMS *Troubridge*, keeping their adrenaline in check. The vessel had left Manfredonia – located on the spur of the Italian boot – at midday and arrived off the target ten hours later. 'The standard of navigation was so high that the destroyer arrived at the exact RV,' remarked the 2SAS report.

The signal was seen, and within half an hour the dories were heading towards the beach on which Laws and Dowell were standing. In one was Cyril Wheeler:

> 'When we actually left the destroyer we were a couple of miles out. The motor dory had the plastic explosives, about 40lbs, yellow stuff that you could mould. With the explosives we had two charges, a cutting charge and a blowing charge. On that raiding party me and Lieutenant Miller were getting the charges and putting the time pencils on.'

Lt Grant Hibbert, left, was one of the first officers to join 2SAS and he proved a quietly efficient leader of men.

In between arriving at the bridge and signalling HMS *Troubridge*, Laws and Dowell had carried out a brief reconnaissance of the target area. There was a house nearby, reportedly a barracks for Carabinieri. Laws crept round the house but was unable to see anything through the curtained windows. Ever so slowly, he tried a door. It opened outwards. He risked a quick peek. Laws counted nineteen Italians, all Carabinieri. He closed the door and then, with Dowell's help, placed a large rock against it, thinking it may impede the Italians for a precious couple of minutes.

The 2SAS raiders reached the beach at fifteen minutes past midnight and were greeted by Lieutenant Laws and Dowell. 'Laws let the demolition party to the bridge and the defence party to the positions which he had selected,' ran *Baobab*'s report. 'The laying of the charges occupied about half an hour. The charge was laid in one strip across the bridge under both tracks from where the ballast was removed.'

Just as Miller finished laying the charges, the Carabinieri realized there was something afoot and the SAS heard shouts and then the sound of a door being broken down. One of the British, Corporal John McGuire, spoke Italian and yelled that they were just a working party carrying out some repairs on the bridge. The report continued:

> 'Meanwhile, the main party had been withdrawn to the dories and Lieutenant Miller was preparing to set off four charges, which had a 10 minute delay, when the Italians opened fire. He completed his task, jumped over the bridge, and returned to the dory. The boats then put out to sea and for the first 400 yards the Italians fired in their direction … the light of a torch directed downwards could be seen as though a search was being made of the bridge.'

'We had to run back down to the beach,' recalled Wheeler. 'We scarpered in the dories by the time they got onto the bridge. But there was a load of shit coming over.' Wheeler remembered Miller scrutinizsing his watch. After ten minutes he looked up expectantly, but there was no thunderous explosion. '[He] looked at his watch and said "it hasn't gone off, we'll have to go back",' recalled Wheeler. 'We thought "you must be joking".' Twelve minutes after Miller had set off the charges, they detonated. The operational report stated:

> 'It resembled the petals of an orange coloured flower opening, while fragments of incandescent material were thrown through the air. It is reasonable to assume that a considerable proportion of the carabinieri were amongst this debris as they were last seen on the bridge. Blue flashes came from the overhead electric power lines which must have also been damaged.'

The raiding party reached HMS *Troubridge* at 0133 hours and the men were hoisted aboard. 'It was a great feeling getting back on board,' said Wheeler. 'They gave us all grog and fags, and we just lay down for a kip.'

The destroyer sailed south, reaching Molfetta without incident on the morning of 31 January. 'When we got back into Molfetta Harbour we returned to our billets, which were in an old bakehouse,' said Wheeler. 'They had rooms where we kipped on the floor in sleeping bags.'

Rations were delivered from Bari, the raiders celebrating the success of the mission with a feast to which some locals were invited.

R.R. BRIDGE 4 MILES N OF FANO

CASMA DI FINANZA

M.A.P.R.C. - 41/·36   : 2-44

A reconnaissance photo used by 2SAS to plan operation Baobab, which resulted in the demolition of a bridge between Ancona and Rimini.

Aerial reconnaissance photographs subsequently revealed that it was six days before engineers were able to make the bridge usable again. In addition, nineteen Carabinieri and fascist militia died in the explosion.

The 2SAS raiding party suffered no casualties. The 'Lessons learned' appendix of the Operational *Baobab* report stated:

1. The operation would have failed had the Navy not been able to navigate with such accuracy.
2. A dress rehearsal was invaluable.
3. Signals worked very satisfactorily and proved that in capable hands [they] contribute[d] considerably to the successful carrying out of an operation.
4. Detailed intelligence work with a model has proved its value.

It had taken more than six months, but Operation *Baobab* was a vindication of everything that Bill Stirling had been telling senior command about the most effective use of the SAS. Previous operations, such as *Chestnut*, *Jonquil* and *Maple*, had been bedevilled by problems caused by a lack of wireless equipment or inefficiency on the part of the Royal Navy. But on *Baobab*, signals had worked well and the Royal Navy had been faultless throughout. The result was the destruction of a bridge, the deaths of several enemy and the safe return of the raiding party.

In April 1945, Major General Richard Gale, commander of the British I Airborne Corps, wrote a report on SAS operations *Maple* and *Baobab* for the War Office. It was a belated report on account of the fact that the twenty-five men on Operation *Maple* had all been either killed or captured; in the spring of 1945, the seventeen who had been captured began returning home after the liberation of their POW camps.

In his summary of *Baobab*, Gale wrote:

> 'Baobab was carried out at short notice but was particularly successful, an important bridge being destroyed with no casualties … . Baobab is interesting as the last of a series of seaborne tasks carried out by the 2nd SAS in Italy and Sicily. It illustrates that for geographically convenient targets the use of sea transport enables a greater quantity of explosive to be carried, and provides a reliable means of withdrawing for the attacking force.'

Chapter Thirteen

On 25 November 1943, the twelve officers and 225 men of the Special Raiding Squadron embarked at Taranto on two LCI troopships for a destination unknown. The weeks since the Battle of Termoli had been idle and frustrating, repeated rumours about returning to Britain being unfounded and adding to the feeling of ennui.

Wherever they were now headed, it wasn't Britain. The ships sailed south, hugging the coast of Italy and then Sicily. On 27 November, the men of the SRS recognized Capo Murro di Porco, where nearly five months earlier they had stormed ashore in their first operation of 1943.

Early the next day, the ships docked at Bizerte in Tunisia, and soon after the SRS boarded a train west for the long journey to Philippeville. 'Moves into 2SAS camp 10 miles outside by 12h30 hours,' noted the SRS war diary on 2 December. 'Good reception. Hot baths. Tents ready. Very pretty countryside in small Bay.'

Some of 2SAS had recently moved back to Philippeville after completing operations in Italy, and it was the first time that the two regiments had formally met. On 4 December, they played each other at rugby, and the next day the rivalry was continued on the football field.

Lieutenant Colonel Bill Stirling and Major Harry Poat went to Algiers for a conference at AFHQ. The men awaited their return eagerly. They were all stuck in limbo, and the hope was the AFHQ would be able to free them, preferably by sending them home. Poat returned from Algiers on 9 December but to the men's disappointment he 'had no griff' (information).

December dragged on. There were more games of rugby, some general training and instruction on weapons and signalling, but the men's hearts weren't in it. On 17 December, 2SAS bought a bullock for Christmas for 18,000

Paddy Mayne proved himself a deft and determined leader of the SRS in Sicily and Italy and was rewarded with a bar to his DSO.

francs (£90), and to the consternation of the SRS they were each asked to contribute 20 francs. The 1SAS took out their anger on their rivals the next day, thrashing them on the rugby field.

Then, on 20 December, the SRS received an order to entrain at short notice. Was this the first stage of their return home? Two days later they were in Algiers, in a transit camp, and that was where they woke on Christmas Day. But there was a hum of excitement in the air; there was a rumour. At 0800 hours, the squadron roll was taken and they were confined to camp. Twelve hours later, a fleet of trucks arrived. 'Climb aboard,' Major Paddy Mayne told his men, 'we're going home.' 'This is really the best way of spending Christmas Day, embarking for UK,' wrote Sergeant Duncan Ridler in the SRS war diary while on the SS *Otranto*. 'All the fear and hope, bad treatment and tolerance of the last two months have ended in something suiting everyone.'

Captain Roy Farran and the rest of 2SAS returned to Philippeville in January 1944 upon completion of operations in Italy. They experienced the same listlessness that had afflicted the SRS the previous month, characterized by Farran as 'the normal run of a regimental soldier's life – squadron football matches, drunken parties, vigorous training … and masses of paperwork'.

The men of 2SAS sailed from North Africa at the end of February, and upon arriving in Britain on 17 March they settled in Monkton, Ayr (the SRS, who had now reverted to 1SAS, were based at Darvel, 15 miles east), to begin training for operations in France.

On 4 April, the SAS Brigade was issued with an operational order by 21st Army Group, responsible for planning the invasion of France. It stated that the

The exact landing spot of the SRS is Augusta is off-limits today but these boulders, seen in 2022, are close and give an idea of what they encountered.

main role of the SAS would be 'attacks on suitable types of objectives in the concentration areas of hostile mobile strategic reserves behind the length of the French Channel coast'. In short, the SAS would parachute into 'an area inland from the coast to a depth of 40 miles' as and when German panzer reserves were observed moving towards the beachhead. It was madness. The SAS were neither trained nor equipped for such a role. It was Lieutenant Colonel Bill Stirling who objected most forcibly. At a conference at HQ Airborne Troops on 5 May, he said that 'to despatch assault parties on general harassing tasks was a misuse of trained troops, who might be used more advantageously in strategic areas'.

Stirling was still bitter about how 2SAS had been misused in Italy, resulting in the capture and deaths of many of his men. On 14 May, Major General Freddie de Guingand (Montgomery's chief of staff) and the American General Harold Bull (assistant chief of staff at SHAEF, the Supreme Headquarters Allied Expeditionary Force) discussed the co-ordination of SAS and resistance group activity at HQ 21 Army Group Rear. During the meeting, de Guingand was informed that 'SAS troops who had operated in Italy felt that they had been badly let down by the failure of the Allies to provide them with any operational bases behind the enemy lines'.

The upshot was that Stirling was sacked as commander of 2SAS in late May and replaced by Lieutenant Colonel Brian Franks. Nevertheless, he won his argument. A new operational order was issued in which the SAS were to be deployed strategically, deep inside France, as Stirling had insisted from the outset.

Farran said of Stirling:

> 'Bill Stirling had a great concept for strategic use of his SAS troops operating in small groups behind the enemy lines in depth. He did realise that if you dropped small parties way behind enemy lines you could cut their lines of communication and cause panic … . [T]he droppings in Sicily were right. A number of SAS had dropped deeper. The landings in the Adriatic to cut bridges and railways and particularly the operation to block the bridge at Rimini [Operation *Baobab*], they were good SAS operations. They were the right ones and eventually later on we did another right one in France.'

For the Special Air Service, 1943 was a pivotal year. It had begun in 'chaos' with the capture of David Stirling and the very real possibility that the regiment would be broken up and the men returned to their parent regiment. That it wasn't, and that one regiment actually became two – and then, in November, the SAS expanded to a brigade – was down to the professionalism, discipline, courage and initiative of the men.

In particular it was the leadership of Bill Stirling and Paddy Mayne that secured the survival of the SAS. Their methods were different and their character contrasting, but they inspired the men under their command and set a standard of excellence to which successive generations of soldiers SAS aspire.

How to use this section

Visiting the areas where the Special Raiding Squadron and 2SAS operated in Sicily and Italy in 1943 is a rich and rewarding experience – particularly for the SRS. In a 1987 interview, Roy Farran remarked: 'Under Paddy Mayne they turned the SAS into commandos and they did very well, but it was not the proper role … . [T]hey succeeded partly because Paddy was a great leader.'

Because the SRS were used as commando troops in Sicily and Italy – the assault force in the vanguard of the infantry invasion – the battlefield tourist can easily pick up their trail. On the other hand, 2SAS operated as small teams of saboteurs, inserting by boat or by parachute and moving rapidly across country. Many of their soldiers were killed or captured, and their movements were therefore not recorded in post-operation reports; some of those who lost their lives did so before German firing squads and there are remote memorials erected by locals in their honour.

Much of where the SAS operated in 1943 has been relatively unspoiled by the passage of time, so it is possible to get a real sense of where they fought and the challenges they faced as they moved inland towards their objective.

There is, however, little signage indicating the historical significance of the area. This may change in Sicily in the coming years as at the time of writing this book an Anglo-American Second World War historical group was in discussions with the powers-that-be to install information boards in many of the sites where the British, Canadians and Americans fought.

In order to help you reach these sites, I've included the GPS coordinates in most cases. To pinpoint the exact location, open Google Maps on your computer/iphone and type in the coordinates shown as decimal degrees, i.e. **47.82479, 2.484187**. A red pin will appear on your screen at the site.

Wherever you go in Sicily and Italy, the people are warm in their welcome – but few speak much English, so be warned.

Most of the sites are accessible by car and then entail just a regular walk around town; but a thorough exploration of Capo Murro di Porco necessitates tramping across knee-high scrub so bring a pair of sturdy walking shoes and wear trousers. It may also be an idea to bring a swimming costume, as there are ample opportunities to swim after exploring the sites – the perfect way to cool off.

Capo Murro di Porco

Paddy Mayne's Special Raiding Squadron first stepped foot on European soil in the early hours of 10 July 1943 when they landed at Capo Murro di Porco. As the crow flies, the northern coast of this stunning peninsula, which is rich in

This is the cottage in Bagnara, photographed in 2022, where Peter Davis and his men were trapped by Germans on the hillside opposite.

history, fauna and wildlife, is less than a mile from the city of Syracuse across the bay.

The objective of the SRS was to neutralize the four guns of a coastal battery situated approximately 100 metres south of the lighthouse (**37.002611, 15.334323**). The plan was for 1 and 2 Troops to land just south of the lighthouse and scale the small cliffs a few metres from the building, while 3 Troop landed half a mile west to strike inland to seize the Damerio farm.

In fact, 1 and 2 Troops came ashore west of their intending landing spot because the captain of the troopship, the *Ulster Monarch*, had sailed closer to the shore than planned and consequently the pilots of the LCAs had their navigation thrown out. 'I never even got my feet wet as we came off the LCA and walked down the ramp on to the rocks,' recalled Sid Payne, who was in Captain Derrick Harrison's section of 2 Troop.

Similarly, Lieutenant Peter Davis, a section leader in 2 Troop, remembered of the landing: 'These were no steep and rugged heights, such as we had trained on … for beyond a sharp climb out of the boats of about five feet, the shore rose gradually ahead of us, in a series of rocky steps and boulders.'

Where 2 Troop landed is approximately at **37.002721, 15.325939**; it is possible to walk down to the water's edge, although it involves negotiating some coral rocks so care is required.

The men of 3 Troop landed a little further west, at approximately **37.003163, 15.320320**, which today is popular with locals as a swimming platform. There are paths leading from the road – the Via degli Zaffiri – to the sea. Capo Murro di Porco is a marine reserve, abundant with plant and fish species, and a magnet for scuba divers.

Once 3 Troop had landed, they moved inland to take Damerio farm, situated on the high ground half a mile from the sea. The original building no longer remains and the property is now private, but it is possible to stand outside the gates and gain a perspective of 3 Troop's movements. Walk back from the sea to the Via degli Zaffiri and turn left, following the road as it bends right (north) onto the SP110, the Strada Capo Murro di Porco. Turn right and then left up the Via Dell Opale, which rises gently uphill, until you reach **37.008957, 15.318959**. Just to the north stood Damerio farm, which Paddy Mayne made his HQ after its capture by 3 Troop.

While 3 Troop had moved inland, 1 and 2 Troops were engaged in neutralizing the coastal battery situated just north of the lighthouse. There is a small car park at **37.004533, 15.332354**, and from there a path leads to the lighthouse, approximately a quarter of a mile to the south. One of the rare information boards on the peninsula is located at the car park on which are marked places of interests such as beaches (including good snorkelling spots in the sea) as well as the site of the second coastal battery on the north of Murro di Porco.

Walk to the lighthouse and then turn so your back is to the sea. The coastal battery is a few hundred metres north-west, located in the scrub, and comprised four guns. Their foundations remain, as do the bunkers where the soldiers slept and where, on the night of 10 July, so did some civilians. When I interviewed SRS veterans in 2002 and 2003, they described firing bursts down the steps into the bunkers, followed by grenades, and then to their horror discovering the bodies of women. It is possible to descend the steps and walk through the bunkers, which have two exits; the scars of battle are clearly visible.

The second gun emplacement is about 50 metres directly north-west of the first, situated on a small rise, and the third is a further 50 metres behind the second. A fourth gun emplacement is 50 metres to the north-east of the second, forming in effect a diamond shape.

The men of 1 Troop, led by Lieutenant Johnny Wiseman's section, made a frontal assault on the guns, as planned, and they had expected 2 Troop to be attacking from the north, i.e. the rear of the Italians. But because 2 Troop was landed to the west, instead of on the east coast, they swept round the left flank of 1 Troop in order to hit the enemy from behind. This led to some confusion, with 1 Troop firing on 2 Troop in the belief they were Italians.

Lieutenant Alex Muirhead's mortar section opened fire on the battery from 750–800 yards, distances that he recorded in his notebook. This suggests that his section landed approximately where 2 Troop came ashore at **37.002721, 15.325939**. Lieutenant Peter Davis recalled hearing the mortars in action close by as he moved towards the target, and appreciating the accuracy of Muirhead and his men. 'The whole objective was most conveniently clearly lit up in every detail,' said Davis, and because of this he realized they were out of position.

Once Sergeant Bill Deakins and his team of engineers had destroyed the four gun emplacements, the SRS believed their task was over. But as they lazed in the early morning sun, looking south at the approach of the main Operation *Husky* invasion fleet and reflecting on a job well done, they heard the boom of guns from further north.

Paddy Mayne assembled his squadron at Damerio farm and ordered an assault on the new threat, which turned out to be an anti-aircraft battery. Nothing remains of this battery, and it is not marked on any official map. In his memoir, it is possible to calculate roughly its whereabouts through clues left by the SAS men who participated in the operation. At **37.030055, 15.302776** is the church of St Mary, the small white church that Lieutenant Peter Davis remembered passing on the approach to the battery. He said that he encountered Harrison's section at the church, and after exchanging pleasantries with the priest, they swung right to attack the battery.

One mile south of the church is the villa of Casa Mallia, **37.019066, 15.315827**, which was used by the SAS as a command post prior to the assault on Battery AS493. The villa is now abandoned but its exterior is as it was in July 1943 and one can understand how its tower gave the SAS a good view of the battery.

Taken in Italy in 2012, Bob Tong salutes his comrades who never came home.

There was a third battery on Capo Murro di Porco and this was situated on the northern tip of the peninsula at Punta Mola, at **37.040770, 15.306963**. This is the only Second World War site marked on the handful of information boards found at Capo Murro, probably because it is also the location of a popular bathing spot. This battery was not attacked by the SRS on 10 July – save for a salvo of shells from the mortar section against an enemy that had already thrown in the towel – and much of it remains, including a brick pillbox. If offers splendid views of Syracuse, just across the bay, and is an ideal location to pause for a picnic after the exertions of exploring Capo Murro di Porco. The beach is small but sandy, and the blue waters of the Ionian Sea are irresistible.

Syracuse War Cemetery

The Special Raiding Squadron suffered only one fatality during the assault on the batteries at Capo Murro di Porco, and that was 22-year-old Geoff Caton. He was from Widnes in the north-west of England and had been a talented boxer in his teens. Caton volunteered for the commandos in 1940 and was posted to No11 Scottish, where among his new comrades were Paddy Mayne and Bill Fraser. Caton was wounded in No11's inaugural operation, a beach assault on the River Litani in Syria in June 1941. After spending several weeks in hospital, Caton volunteered for the SAS in early 1942 and he took part in several raids in Libya in the autumn of that year. Caton was a popular member of the squadron, and the manner of his death enraged his comrades. 'We were now passing the trooper who had been shot so treacherously when taking prisoners under the cloak of a white flag,' remembered Bill Deakins, of that morning on Capo Murro di Porco. Caton was being treated by medics, and Deakins, 'having known him very well', enquired how he was. 'With a wry smile, he said he had been one of the unlucky ones,' said Deakins. 'Wishing him luck and that I would see him on his return, I passed along. I was told later that he had passed away within half an hour of our conversation, having been severely wounded in the top of the thigh.'

Caton is buried in Syracuse war cemetery, which is situated on the western outskirts of the city at **37.074681, 15.257941**. His plot can be found in the cemetery register situated at the entrance. Also buried here are John Bentley

The coastal battery and one of the bunkers on Cape Murro di Porco as seen in 2023.

and George Shaw, who lie side by side. Sadly, the two medics, who were attached to the SRS from the Royal Army Medical Corps, may well have been the medics attending to Caton when Deakins passed by. Bentley and Shaw were killed in the first minutes of the landing at Augusta on 12 July. On their headstones is the date 13 July, but this is incorrect; the SRS landed in the early evening of the 12th, and I spoke to several veterans who recalled seeing Bentley and Shaw hit as they scrambled across the rocks. 'He was bending over a colleague when all of a sudden he collapsed to the ground,' said Alf Dignum of Shaw. 'I just got out of the way quick and hoped I wasn't next. Having a wireless strapped to you back doesn't exactly help matters.'

Bear in mind that the cemetery is on a busy road and there is no car park.

The SRS marched into Syracuse from Capo Murro di Porco, and later that day sailed on the *Ulster Monarch* to Augusta. Although there is nothing specifically connected to the SRS in Syracuse, it would be remiss of any visitor to Sicily to neglect this remarkable city, which is listed by UNESCO as a World Heritage Site. Nearly 3,000 years old, it is teeming with Greek and Roman history, not to mention, for those of a more modern bent, many wonderful harbourside restaurants serving local delicacies. An ideal place to recharge!

Augusta

To follow in the wake of the SRS on that July evening, take the E45 north from Syracuse, signposted Catania and Augusta. Major Harry Poat, second-in-command of the SRS, described Augusta as a 'strangely shaped little peninsula', and he was right. An important naval port in 1943, it is constructed on a spit of land attached to the mainland by a bridge, which is overshadowed by an austere and formidable citadel. Beyond the citadel is a large public garden leading to the 'old town', now a residential and shopping district. It was on the southern tip of the old town that the SRS landed at approximately 2000 hours on 12 July.

Today, this area is an Italian naval base and, being a restricted military zone, out of bounds to the public. Therefore, it is not possible to stand on the exact spot where the SRS landed, under heavy fire from the Germans sited on the high ground to the north. However, if one skirts the edge of the naval base heading east, through a housing estate, one comes to the water's edge, at **37.219886, 15.226547**, only 100 metres or so from where the SRS came ashore. The boulders here are similar to the ones the SRS negotiated as they dashed from their LCAs. 'As we stumbled over the slippery rocks, bullets chip into the ground around us and someone from the previous wave yells at us to get into single file,' wrote Davis. 'Bent low, we double through a small gap to find ourselves in a narrow street, sheltered temporarily at least, from the watching eyes across the water.'

Those narrow streets have been replaced by ugly high rises, but nonetheless one can easily pick up the trail of the SRS as they moved north-west, grateful to be out of sight of the German fire. The road you want is the main thoroughfare in the old town, the Via Principe Umberto, **37.229749, 15.220343**, now lined with shops and bars. It was on the night of 12 July, but the windows were smashed and sniper fire was a menace for the men, who moved from doorway to doorway. Eventually they reached the top of the Via Principe Umberto, and before them saw the large public garden, **37.232386, 15.220321**, a popular meeting place in more peaceful times. It was here that Major Paddy Mayne set

The view south from the foundations of one of the coastal guns at Cape Murro di Porco.

up his command post at the southern edge of the garden; he soon left Harry Poat in charge and continued north with 1 and 3 Troop.

There is plenty of parking on the southern edge of the garden, should one wish to continue on foot, but it's possible to drive over the original bridge, **37.236041, 15.220164**, that the SRS crossed. The new bridge at **37.237610, 15.223854**, along which one enters the old town today, is visible across the water. Also unmissable is what the SRS described as a citadel but is actually a medieval castle constructed in the 1230s on the orders of Frederick II of Swabia, at **37.234385, 15.220258**. The foundations of the castle were built directly on the underlying rock. Post-war, it served as a time for a prison but has long since been abandoned; to the anger of many, this historic masterpiece is falling into ruin and is consequently closed to the public.

Once over the old bridge, continue north to the railway station, **37.243694, 15.218221**, which was an objective for 3 Troop. One section remained in the

George Shaw and John Bentley were killed at Augusta and lie side by side in Syracuse cemetery.

stationmaster's office while the rest of the troop continued to advance towards the crossroads at **37.249515, 15.219422**, now a roundabout, although they didn't quite get that far.

One section, led by Captain Ted Lepine, had a fire-fight with a German patrol. 'Out of the darkness on the other side of the wall came a patrol of Germans,' said Albert Youngman. 'We filed past each other. We weren't sure who they were and neither were they. They got about 20 yards past us before "Snowy" Kirk let go with the bren gun and got them.' This contact probably occurred around **37.245502, 15.217838**.

Meanwhile, back at the stationmaster's office, one of 3 Troop made the mistake of answering the telephone. Three minutes later, shells began to crash in and around the station.

During the night of 12/13 July, Paddy Mayne withdrew his men back across the old bridge to the high ground around the citadel and public garden. They expected a German counter-attack, but it never materialized. Instead, the troops and tanks that appeared not long before dawn belonged to the British 17 Brigade.

The SRS were stood down, and that was when the party began with many soldiers doing their best to drink Augusta dry. The party HQ was in the public

The railway line at Termoli in 2023. Eighty years earlier the SAS were positioned on this high ground and repelled countless Nazi attacks down the line.

garden, and Sergeant Bill Deakins recalled that 'a piano had been salvaged from a damaged cafe, and someone able to play with some gusto and style, was joined by others. Their contributions, the singing of popular ballads, raucous and ribald songs, many of them sung blasphemously to popular hymn tunes … impromptu dancing, steps and antics never seen before or since.' If one stands in the public garden under the trees on a sultry summer's day, one can almost hear the SRS revelry.

Bagnara, Italy

The Special Raiding Squadron landed late on Bagnara, coming ashore two-and-a-half hours behind schedule in the early hours of 4 September. Eleven miles south, the main British invasion force was establishing a beachhead at Reggio.

The SRS's orders were to seize and hold Bagnara to facilitate the advance north. Founded in the Middle Ages at the foot of a terraced hillside facing the Tyrrhenian Sea, Bagnara had suffered widespread damage in two earthquakes in the eighteenth and nineteenth centuries. In the twentieth century, it began to establish a reputation as a holiday resort with its long sandy beach.

The first wave of the SRS landed at Bagnara in four LCAs at 0445 hours, and 3 Troop and B and C Sections of 1 Troop occupied the beach and wide

Charlie Tobin was killed at Bagnara and buried on the other side of Italy in Bari CWGC.

promenade without encountering any opposition. There was a problem, however; they should have landed on the southern extremity of the beach, but instead they had come ashore at the northern end, nearly a mile out of position. This inaccuracy, coupled with the two hour-plus delay, forced Major Paddy Mayne into a change of plan, as his second-in-command explained to Lieutenant Peter Davis as they crouched behind the stone wall that separated the beach from the promenade. 'Paddy has decided to alter the whole plan because we have been landed so late and so far out of position,' said Poat. 'We have no time to clear the town properly now, and we certainly don't want to find ourselves caught in it in daylight, so we will push straight through, and hold the bridge which crosses a deep wadi bed at the foot of the main road running up the mountain to the north of the town.'

The instructions for 3 Troop were unchanged, and they moved south to secure the railway station and tunnel, at **38.282778, 15.800367**.

Where Poat and Davis had their hurried conflab is approximately at **38.291188, 15.807625**. Davis led his section inland, followed by that of Captain Derrick Harrison, who wrote an evocative description of their route through town and up towards the bridge, Pont di Caravilla, at **38.289166, 15.807571**. 'We slipped into town, padding along silently in our rubber soles,' he remembered. 'Almost immediately the buildings began to take shape through the grey dawn haze … the street along which we were advancing led straight inland. At the far end a long flight of broad stone steps led upwards towards the church, like a picture of an Aztec temple.'

The best way to follow in the footsteps of 2 Troop is, logically, on foot. The church is the Maria Santtissima del Rosario, at **38.286923, 15.806653**, and the street up which Davis and Harrison led their men is the Via Maria Santtissima del Rosario, at **38.288771, 15.804194**. Upon reaching the church, turn left, as 2 Troop did, walking up the Piazza Rosario, **38.287013, 15.807029**, on to the main road that leads from Bagnara up into the hills, the SS18. The bridge is up ahead, but when Harrison's section began heading in its direction at dawn on 4 September, they heard the

Bob Tong at the graveside of Philip Pinckney at Florence CWGC in 2012. The exact circumstances of Pinckney's death remain a mystery.

sound of other marching boots in their rear. 'The Germans were round the corner, in a cloud of dust,' he recalled, '… blissfully unaware that we were other than Italians.'

The Germans were engineers who had marched overnight from their main defensive position south of the railway tunnel at **38.281426, 15.798394**, and they were on their way to blow the bridge just a few hundred metres away. They had no idea that the British had landed an hour or so earlier. Harrison's section ambushed the Germans just as they came round the corner of the road, approximately at **38.287121, 15.807215**.

Brian Franks, left, brigade major of the Special Service Brigade, at the battle for Termoli replaced Bill Stirling as 2SAS C.O in 1944.

Peter Davis recalled that, having been alerted by Harrison that they had company, he led his men up some stone steps into a position overlooking the main road, from where they joined Harrison's section in attacking the unsuspecting Germans. This may be at **38.287668, 15.807557**. According to Davis, about thirty prisoners were taken.

Upon reaching the bridge, which was held by 1 Troop, Davis's section continued on the SS18, negotiating the many hairpin bends. Today, anyone ascending this road on foot must keep an eye out for traffic; for the SRS, the threat was from the Germans. In his memoir, Davis recalled his anxiety as they advanced down the most exposed stretch of the road, which ran straight for 300 yards, at approximately **38.286356, 15.811705**. They padded along in bright early-morning sunshine, ascending the road and edging closer all the time to the German positions. 'So anxious were we feeling about the exposed and vulnerable stretch of road along which we had to pass, that we were almost expecting the trouble when it came,' wrote Davis. A salvo of mortar bombs landed just behind Davis's sub-section and in front of the section led by Sergeant Bill Mitchell. The latter withdrew back down the road, but Davis yelled his men forwards. 'We doubled like mad things down that road, in a vain search for cover from those murderous eyes on the hillside above,' said Davis. 'We rounded a slight right-hand bend as the bullets started to chip into the asphalt beside us, our pleading eyes frantically searching for some trace of cover. And there, barely 50 yards ahead, was the most wonderful sight we could wish for. It was a small one-roomed peasant cottage, on the left side of the road.'

Thanks to Davis's vivid description, it is possible to put oneself in his place, following the right-hand bend, at **38.287061, 15.814796**, and then seeing the peasant cottage, which eighty years later is still there, at **38.287574, 15.815686**. So too is the 'tall cactus plant', on the western side of the house, which Davis sheltered behind having reached the cottage unscathed. Davis and his twelve men spent nearly ten hours cowering in this cottage, pinned down by German machine-gun and mortar fire. This, he said, came from 'less than 200 yards ahead, at the point where the road crossed a deep gully, it doubled back to the left at an acute angle to the stretch up which we had come, and rising all the time, it ran almost parallel to us along the far side of the valley, before finally disappearing from view around the shoulder of the mountain away over to our left'. The SS18 is exactly as Davis described it all those years ago, and if one continues along it for a quarter of a mile from the cottage, at **38.288021, 15.817992**, one gets a good sense of why the Germans were able to pin down the thirteen men from the SRS.

At one point in the day, two men – Sergeant Andy Storey and Private Charlie Tobin – volunteered to try to reach a culvert that ran under the road and led down the hillside. To reach it, however, meant a dash out of the door that faced the German position to the path that led down to the culvert. The culvert is visible if one continues on the road to where the Germans were dug in, at **38.287893, 15.818041**.

Storey was first out of the door, and then Tobin; Storey made it, but Tobin was shot dead. As soon as night fell, the men withdrew, but not before Davis had found Tobin's body a few yards down the path. He had been hit by a burst in the chest. Davis removed his rifle and personal belongings and then led his section back down the road.

After the Germans had withdrawn from Bagnara, Davis walked back to the cottage accompanied by Tobin's best friend, Corporal Bob Lowson. They buried Tobin on the hillside just below the cottage. 'When I got back down the lads were all asleep on the railway station,' remembered Lowson. 'In the corner was an Italian local with a little squeezebox playing Amapola. I could have bloody cried.'

Bari War Cemetery

Charlie Tobin is buried in the Commonwealth War Graves cemetery at Bari, at **41.064916, 16.894335**, 5 miles south from the centre of Bari. There is parking in front of the cemetery, which contains 2,128 Commonwealth burials from the Second World War. Buried with Tobin in Bari are three of the five SRS men killed at Bagnara: Thomas Parris, Charlie Richards and William Howell, who were all signallers.

When the Special Raiding Squadron were resting in billets at Gallico, squadron sergeant major Graham Rose wrote to the families of the five men killed during the recent operation. To John and Eve Howell, parents of William Kitchener Howell (born in September 1916, three months after the death of Lord Kitchener), he wrote:

> 'It is with great regret and my deepest sympathy that I have to inform you of the death in action of your son, William Kitchener. As his squadron sergeant major I feel it is my duty to write and tell you of the manner in which he met his death and of how much he will be missed by his comrades in this unit. "Bill", as he was known to us all, came to the squadron some time in May as a troop signaller. At that time we were training hard for a big operation and your son worked well and hard, soon becoming a valuable addition to the squadron ... . [I]t was during the invasion of Italy that he met his untimely end but I can assure you, in the hope that it will bring you some small comfort, that he passed away quietly and without pain. Your great loss is shared by the entire squadron. Bill was more than liked by the boys and many is the time that I have listened and laughed at his imitations of Maurice

Photographed from Termoli old town, the harbour was where German aircraft divebombed 2SAS as they arrived in a schooner to reinforce their SRS comrades.

Chevalier. Always smiling, always ready to help anyone at any time, he leaves a gap in the ranks that can never be filled.

'His personal effects will be forwarded to you at our earliest convenience together with the unit badge which is inscribed "Who Dares Wins". I pass on to you the condolences and sympathy of his commanding officer, officers and other ranks in this moment of your great bereavement. We pay homage to the memory of a brave soldier and a gentleman.

'I beg to remain, yours sincerely, Graham Rose.'

The inscription on Howell's headstone reads: 'In loving memory of our dear Bill. He died that we might live.'

The fifth member of the SRS who was killed at Bagnara, Lance Bombardier John Ball, was buried at Salerno cemetery, at **40.625716, 14.921215**. He had been wounded fighting with 1 Troop on 4 September and died from his wounds in a field ambulance. He was aged 20. 'Happy and smiling, always content. Loved and respected wherever he went' is the inscription on Ball's headstone.

Termoli

It would be a shame not to visit the attractive and bustling city of Bari, home for a brief period to 2SAS in September 1943 before they left to head north to Termoli, by boat in the case of B Squadron and by jeep for Roy Farran and D Squadron.

From Bari to Termoli today it is a straightforward drive up the E55 for 135 miles. There is plenty of parking in Termoli, which has expanded extensively since the Second World War. The most attractive part of town is also the oldest, at **42.004610, 14.997393**, built on a promontory overlooking the Adriatic Sea, with narrow cobbled streets and several old and evocative buildings that conjure up the past. The harbour is on the eastern side of the promontory, and it was here on the morning of 5 October that German fighter bombers attacked the schooner and caiques containing the officers and men of B Squadron, 2SAS. The only SAS fatality was 33-year-old Arthur Dench, batman to Captain Simon Baillie. Baillie subsequently wrote to Dench's widow, Marjorie, saying that 'the harbour was dive-bombed and unfortunately the boat, on which your husband was on board while looking after some stores received a direct hit, and sank like a stone'.

Dench's body was not recovered and he is commemorated on the Cassino Memorial, located within the Cassino war cemetery, at **41.477070, 13.825869**.

To the west of the old town is the main beach at Termoli, a vast sandy expanse that stretches west for miles. One has a wonderful view of the beach standing by the western wall of the old town, and it was approximately at **42.005276, 14.990701** where the Special Service Brigade landed in the early hours of 3 October 1943.

Lieutenant John Tonkin of 3 Troop led his B Section south-east towards the bridge over the River Biferno, at **41.961099, 15.026982**. However, en route they encountered the Germans withdrawing, and most of the SRS were captured at around **41.988450, 14.998168**, though this is an approximation. Private Alex Griffiths recalled trying to escape by hiding among some bushes in a hollow, what he described as a dry river bed.

This part of Termoli has changed considerably in the last eighty years (there was barely a suburb to the town in the war) and it is hard to be exact when following the route of 3 Troop.

The same is true of the other two troops. A map drawn by 2 Troop's Lieutenant Peter Davis shortly after the end of the war indicated that they were a mile or south of Tonkin's 3 Troop section, around **41.927316, 14.989382**, but this does not fit with the SRS war diary account of the operation, which stated that it was 1 Troop which advanced down the Termoli to Campomarino road, close on the heels of 3 Troop.

The men of 2 Troop advanced south towards the village of Ponticelli on what today is the SS483, and Davis's B Section reached as far as San Giacomo, at **41.963731, 14.941618**, before being ordered to withdraw north because the village was going to be shelled. Captain Derrick Harrison's B Section reported seeing Germans digging in half a mile west of San Giacomo.

Davis's section spent the night of 3/4 October in a barn, north-east of San Giacomo, somewhere in the vicinity of **41.969401, 14.958558**, out of radio contact with the rest of the SRS, which had withdrawn in the afternoon of 3 October to the monastery in the belief that the battle for Termoli had been won.

The monastery was in the Via Regina Margherita di Savoia, at **42.003214, 14.995331**, a street that was opposite a public garden. The public garden is now a car park and the monastery is a public building. During the battle for Termoli, the monastery was a comfortable billet for the SRS, a respite from the fighting outside. But in the afternoon of 5 October, five trucks pulled up in the Via Regina Margherita di Savoia and Nos 1 and 2 Troop were ordered to board them and reinforce the western perimeter of the town as the German counter-attack intensified. The last truck in the convoy received a direct hit from a shell, killing all but two of Johnny Wiseman's section in 1 Troop: himself and Reg Seekings. Some of 2 Troop dived for cover in the public garden before emerging ono the street to try to help their comrades. The trucks were facing (south) up the Via Regina Margherita di Savoia, away from the sea, and the vehicle that was hit was opposite what is today a pharmacy, at **42.002971, 14.995296**.

The survivors from the shelling moved west to reinforce 3 Troop and one section of 2 Troop (about sixty SRS in total) who had just withdrawn north to take up position on the lip of the railway embankment with their backs to the sea, at approximately **42.005234, 14.984192**. Roy Farran and his men from 2SAS were positioned on the other side (south) of the embankment, facing west, at **42.004327, 14.987036**, in the expectation that the Germans would attack down the railway line, which they did, only to be beaten back by heavy and accurate fire from Bren guns. The SRS HQ Squadron, together with the mortar section, were at the railway station, at **42.000940, 14.991900**, a couple of hundred metres east.

Had the Germans pressed their attack during the evening of 5 October, they might have broken through the thinly stretched British defences, but the fierce fighting of the last twenty-four hours had shaken them and cost them many casualties. The arrival on the evening of 5 October of 38 (Irish) Brigade closed the window of opportunity for the Germans. By dawn on the 6th, four Sherman tanks had moved into position in the railway goods yards on the left flank of 2SAS, at **42.002707, 14.989887**. Further south was a squadron of Shermans from the Canadian 1 Armoured Brigade.

On the most western perimeter of the British defences was a troop from No40 RM Commando and a sub-section of SRS from 3 Troop, buttressed by some 6-pdr anti-tank field guns that had been brought up the previous evening and were crewed by the 56th Reconnaissance Regiment. They passed the night of 5/6 October positioned in and around the cemetery at **42.003860, 14.980849**, but at 0500 hours they came under heavy shelling, mortar and small-arms fire and withdrew. At 1000 hours, German mortar fire from a house close to the cemetery killed Captain Sandy Wilson and Lance Corporal Bob Scherzinger, but a short while afterwards the 2nd London Irish Rifles advanced, supported by the commandos and 3 Troop SRS, and the cemetery was retaken. The Canadian Shermans to the south also drove the Germans back, and by 1300 hours the high ground to the west of Termoli was in Allied hands and the battle was effectively over.

Sangro War Cemetery

Wilson and Scherzinger are commemorated on the Casino Memorial to those servicemen who were killed in Sicily and Italy and have no known grave. They include Major Geoffrey Appleyard, second-in-command of 2SAS, whose plane was shot down over Sicily on the night of 12/13 July, and Captain John Gunston and his seven men from Operation *Maple Driftwood*, who were either drowned and/or executed in March 1943.

The other nineteen men from the Special Raiding Squadron who lost their lives at Termoli are buried in Sangro war cemetery, at **42.219164, 14.536533,** 30 miles north of Termoli on the E55. Among them is Private Alexander Skinner, killed on the truck, who had been awarded a Military Medal for his courage and fortitude at Capo Murro di Porco. Two other MM holders were killed in the same incident, Chris O'Dowd and Bill McNinch. McNinch was a popular Glaswegian, the squadron comedian, and the inscription on his headstone reads: 'Where Willie McNinch sleeps in peace until the dawn. 1939–43.'

Other places of interest

Florence War Cemetery
Three members of 2SAS are buried in Florence, all of them members of Operation *Speedwell*: Captain Philip Pinckney, who disappeared from the DZ at the start of the operation on 7 September and whose fate has never been conclusively determined, and Captain Pat Dudgeon and Gunner Bernard Brunt, who were caught and executed on 3 October. The inscription on Brunt's headstone reads: 'There's a face that is always with us. There's a voice we long to hear. Adieu.' The cemetery is a couple of miles east of Florence, at **43.769909, 11.343036**.

There is also a memorial to Brunt and Littlejohn in the Cisa Pass in Tuscany, at **44.469465, 9.931505**, close to the spot where they were caught. The pair were shot a few hours later.

Staglieno War Cemetery, Genoa
The other two members of Operation *Speedwell* executed were Sergeant Bill Foster and Corporal James Shortall. They are buried in a joint grave at Staglieno cemetery at Genoa, at **44.430064, 8.950962,** and there is a memorial to them at the site of their execution, just east of Ponzano Magra, at **44.142424, 9.944171**.

Assisi War Cemetery
Anthony Widdrington is buried at Assisi cemetery, at **43.046593, 12.609312**, about 10 miles south-east of where he died, on Sant Egidio airfield, at **43.094155, 12.500182**. The inscription on his headstone reads: '*Joye Sans Fin*' (Joy without end).

Glossary

1SAS	Designated First Special Air Service Regiment on 28 September 1942, it was formed from L Detachment, under the command of Lieutenant Colonel David Stirling.
2SAS	Designated First Special Air Service Regiment on 13 May 1943, it was commanded by Lieutenant Colonel Bill Stirling.
A Force	A sub-section of Military Intelligence Section 9 of the War Office. The Mediterranean branch of A Force, codenamed N Section, had the task in 1943 of rescuing the large number of Allied POWs.
AFHQ	Allied Force Headquarters, in control of Allied operational forces in the Mediterranean theatre from August 1942 until May 1945.
Albemarle	A twin-engine aircraft used by the RAF for transport and aerial reconnaissance.
Bren gun	Czech-made light machine gun with a range of 2,000 yards (1,800 metres).
CCO	Chief of Combined Operations, in charge of directing Combined Operations Headquarters to attack the enemy by means of raids carried out by use of combined naval and army forces.
CGS	Chief of the General Staff, who, in Middle East Command, answered to the Commander-in-chief.
Cyrenaica	The wartime eastern coastal region of Libya. Cyrenaica bordered Tripolitania in the north-west and Fezzan in the south-west.
DCM	Distinguished Conduct Medal, the equivalent of the DSO – second only to the VC – awarded to NCOs and other ranks.

DCO	Director of Combined Operations, responsible for planning commando raids. Sir Roger Keyes was the first DCO in July 1940.
DSO	Distinguished Service Order, awarded for meritorious or distinguished service by wartime officers.
DZ	Drop zone for paratroopers and supplies.
Folboat	Collapsible canoes made of canvas on a wooden frame.
Gestapo	Geheime Staatspolizei: the secret police force of Nazi Germany.
GHQ	General Headquarters, Cairo, also known as Middle East Headquarters (MEHQ).
Jeep	The American Willys jeep that was first used by the SAS in July 1942 in the North African campaign.
LCA	Landing Craft, Assault, 40ft vessels capable of holding thirty-five soldiers and used for amphibious operations.
LCI	Landing Craft, Infantry, vessels capable of holding up to 210 equipped soldiers', LCIs had a crew of twenty-four and were 160ft in length.
LRDG	Long Range Desert Group, formed in June 1940 by Ralph Bagnold.
MC	Military Cross, awarded for outstanding gallantry in the face of the enemy, to captains or officers of lower rank.
MM	Military Medal, awarded for outstanding gallantry in the face of the enemy to NCOs or other ranks.
MTB	Motor Torpedo Boat, a small fast vessel used by the Royal Navy.
NCO	Non-commissioned officer.
POW	Prisoner of war.
RTU	Returned to Unit, the fate of special forces soldiers who failed the selection course.
SBS	Special Boat Squadron, formed in March 1943 under the command of George Jellicoe. Not to be confused with the Special Boat Section, raised by Roger Courtney in 1940, which served with distinction in the Mediterranean and the Far East.

Schmeisser	The MP40 machine pistol was designed in Germany in 1938 by Heinrich Vollmer, not Hugo Schmeisser, but was known by Allied troops as the Schmeisser.
SOE	Special Operations Executive, formed in 1940 to conduct espionage and sabotage in occupied territory.
SRS	Special Raiding Squadron, formed in 1943 from 1SAS and reverted to that regiment at the end of the year.
SS	Schutzstaffel: the paramilitary force of Nazi Germany.
STC	The Special Training Centre, Lochailort, established in June 1940 under the direction of Bill Stirling and Simon Fraser, Lord Lovat.
Vickers K	Rapid-firing machine gun designed for aircraft and later used by the SAS.

Index